BE STRONG

Daily Devotional for Men

ADISAN Publishing AB

Mr. Anders Bennett

Table of Contents

Introduction

Everyday life and responsibilities, meeting expectations, leading, and fighting for truth, overcoming challenges need a constant alignment with who we are and our path. "Be Strong" is that source of spiritual orientation, a daily inspiration that would keep you going.

Use this devotional to strengthen the core of your life and faith. Trust God's plan for you and faithfully follow it.

It has a carefully chosen bible verse, a short explanation, and a prayer for each day of the year. Meditate and reflect upon each day's scripture.

You can start on any day of the Year as the devotions are numbered day 1, day 2, and so on.

We hope that this devotional assists men in learning more about God and develop a Godly character.

Strong Men

Prepare

Be Strong in the Lord

> *"Finally, be strong in the Lord . . . "*
> **EPHESIANS 6:10**

After a challenging letter to the church in Ephesus, Paul gives this final encouragement to "be strong in the Lord." What does this mean? What kind of strength is Paul referring to? Surely, it's not physical strength because the church is full of all different kinds of people: men and women, young and old, healthy and sick. The strength he is referring to is inner strength. It is steadfastness. Like a boulder in a rushing river, it will not be moved.

This is the kind of strength we will study and think through as we journey together through the Bible. We will look at various men in Scripture who have shown this strength. We will see similar commands and consider how to live them out. We will behold our Savior, Jesus, who is both the example and foundation of our strength. Together, we will learn what strong men do.

Dear God, there are days where I feel so weak. I need Your strength. Help me to learn how to be strong in the Lord. Amen.

In His Strength

> *". . . and in the strength of his might. "*
> EPHESIANS 6:10

Where does this unwavering inner strength come from? It comes from the "strength of *His* might." Jesus is the source of our strength. Friend, this is an infinite resource! He is a well that will not run dry! It doesn't come from meditation practices, workout routines, or protein shakes. It comes from our God, the creator of the universe!

We will examine 13 different things that strong men do over the next year, but we cannot forget where the strength to do these things comes from. Praise God that we don't have to be strong enough by ourselves. It's not up to us! We don't have to rely on our own efforts. We have a strong God who is mighty to save us and desires to strengthen us day by day.

Dear God, I praise You for You are a mighty God. There is no one like You. No one else is powerful to save. Amen.

Suit Up

> *"Put on the whole armor of God, that you may be able to stand against the schemes of the devil. "*
> **EPHESIANS 6:11**

Immediately after giving the command to be strong in the Lord, Paul explains how we are to do that. He starts by telling us to put on the whole armor of God. This means war! There is a battle to be fought, an enemy to overcome, and attacks to be endured. Therefore, we must suit up! A football player has pads, a boxer has gloves, and we have the armor of God.

This can be intimidating and nerve-wracking. If you've spent time in a locker room before a big game, you can relate to these feelings. There is excitement and fear rolled into one. Be encouraged! God has not sent you to war without armor. He hasn't left you ill-equipped to handle the challenges ahead. He has given you Himself, His armor, and His strength. So daily, we must put on the whole armor of God if we are to be victorious.

———— ✦ ————

Dear God, thank you for not sending me into battle alone. You have given me all that I need. Amen.

———— ✦ ————

Know Your Enemy

> *"For we do not wrestle against flesh and blood, but against the rulers, against the authorities, against the cosmic powers over this present darkness, against the spiritual forces of evil in the heavenly places. "*
> EPHESIANS 6:12

A key to winning a war is knowing your enemy. If your enemy has 10,000 soldiers equipped with guns of various calibers, then your army cannot show up to the fight on horseback with swords in hand. In this verse, Paul gives us a clear picture of our enemy. He begins by saying who it is not. It is not other people. This doesn't mean you won't have physical enemies along the way; it means that ultimately, our enemy is bigger than that. Our fight is against the Devil and his demons that we fight.

This is not a challenge to take lightly.

Our enemy is vicious and cunning. He "prowls about like a roaring lion, seeking someone to devour." In the beginning, in the Garden of Eden, he was there, tempting Adam and Eve to sin. As promised in the Garden, "he shall crush your head, and you shall bruise his heel." Jesus will win this war. In His strength, we will fight.

Dear God, my enemy is fierce and strong. But You, O Lord, are stronger. I trust You to fight for me, Amen.

Stand Firm

> *"Therefore take up the whole armor of God,*
> *that you may be able to withstand in the evil day,*
> *and having done all, to stand firm."*
> EPHESIANS 6:13

Stand firm. Dig your heels in. Be in a ready position. Paul is about to explain what the armor of God is. Before he does, he reminds us that our posture is one of strength and endurance. Wars aren't won easily or overnight. There will be pressure to fall back. Paul tells us to stand firm.

All of us have the natural instinct of fight or flight. When situations get hard, we either desire to run away or run into the fire. Rather than run away or run towards the fight, Paul's encouragement is to remain in place. As a Viking warrior in a shield wall, our job at first is to hold the line. In your life, don't give up ground to the Devil. Don't give in to "small" sins or temptations. Also, don't go looking for a fight. Venturing into places where sin and temptation normally find you is dangerous. Stand firm.

Dear God, Help me to stand firm. There are so many things trying to bring me down. Give me strength, Amen.

The Belt of Truth

"Stand therefore, having fastened on the belt of truth . . ."
EPHESIANS 6:14

Now Paul begins to show us the armor of God, and he begins with the belt of truth. Here is where cultural and historical context will give a lot of insight into what he means. For the average person in biblical times, his everyday outfit was a long robe. As you can imagine, this is not the ideal attire for a warrior! Before battle would begin, they would wrap the lower half of their robe around their waist and hold it there with a belt. The belt was the first step towards readiness.

For the man who is strong in the Lord, our belt is one of truth. Jesus teaches us that God's word is truth (John 17:17). We must prepare ourselves for the battle by gathering together the loose thoughts in our minds and tightening them down with the Bible. Regularly reading the Bible, devotions, and Christian books helps to keep ourselves ready to fight.

Dear God, I need your word to be prepared for battle. Show me Your truth. In Jesus' name, Amen.

The Breastplate of Righteousness

". . . and having put on the breastplate of righteousness, "
Ephesians 6:14

There are two important things to understand about the breastplate. The first is that it covers your most vital organ, your heart. The second is that it is only meant to protect your breast and not your back. This armor assumes the attacker is striking to kill and that the wearer is not going to run.

Why is it, then, that righteousness is the material of the breastplate? Satan's lies and temptations cannot pierce this kind of armor. The problem for us is that there is no one righteous, no, not even one (Romans 3:10). This is why it's called the armor of God. It is the righteousness of Jesus, given to us by faith, that protects us (2 Corinthians 5:21).

Dear God, thank You for the great gift of Your righteousness. Help us to wear Your armor with confidence amid temptation. Amen.

The Shoes of the Gospel

> *"and, as shoes for your feet, having put on the readiness given by the gospel of peace."*
> EPHESIANS 6:15

When you think of armor, you probably don't think of shoes. Your mind probably started with thoughts of a shield, helmet, or even the breastplate. With a command to stand firm before the armor, your shoes hold a higher value. What will allow you to dig in? What will help you hold your ground? The gospel of peace.

The gospel of peace is the incredible story of Jesus' perfect life, sacrificial death, and victorious resurrection. I encourage you to give all you have to understand the implications of this gospel on your life. It is a sure foundation (Matthew 7:24). With these shoes, you will not be shaken. You can stand in confidence because by the gospel, you have peace with God (Romans 5:1).

Dear God, remind me to put on the shoes of the gospel every day. It is in your peace that I stand and in Your strength that I fight. Amen.

The Shield of Faith

> "*In all circumstances take up the shield of faith,
> with which you can extinguish all the flaming
> darts of the evil one*"
> EPHESIANS 6:16

The shield of faith is the first piece of armor that Paul mentions that is not something you wear. It's something you hold out in front of you. It's like armor for your armor. So what is this first line of defense for us as Christians? It is our faith in God.

This is also the first piece of armor that is directly connected to the attack of the Devil. This sheds light on what we can expect. Satan will shoot darts at us, and the first thing to take the hit is our faith. Think about it. How can the devil convince you to run and make your breastplate useless? How can he loosen your footing in the gospel? How can he remove the belt of truth that prepares you for battle? He can sow doubt, and doubt is the enemy of faith. Brother, hold firmly to this shield!

Dear God, there are days where I lack faith. This tempts me to run from the fight. Give me faith, O God. Amen.

The Helmet of Salvation

"and take the helmet of salvation. . ."
EPHESIANS 6:17

Now we come to the last piece of the armor of God - the helmet of salvation. Once again, we see the armor dripping with the gospel. We find our salvation and highest protection in the gospel of Jesus Christ. If you look at the armor as a whole, you will see that we are fully protected by the life, death, and resurrection of Jesus.

In Christ, we find the belt of truth (John 14:6). Through Jesus, we are given our righteousness. It is in His gospel that we stand against the devil's lies. And it is by faith in this gospel that we are first protected. Now we see that the salvation that comes by grace through faith protects our minds. If you want to take up the armor of God, you must repent and believe in the gospel!

Dear God, I need Jesus. He is my rock and salvation. Help me to trust in Him today. Amen.

⇒ Day 11 ⇐

The Sword of the Spirit

> *"...and the sword of the Spirit,*
> *which is the word of God."*
> Ephesians 6:17

In this verse, Paul introduces the one and the only weapon we have: the sword of the Spirit. He leaves no guesswork for us. He tells us plainly, "which is the word of God." Our weapon against our sinful flesh, the enticing world, and the deceptive devil is the sure word of God.

This is the weapon that Jesus Himself uses when he is tempted in the wilderness (Luke 4:4). The writer of Hebrews describes the sword as "living and active . . . piercing to the division of soul and of spirit, of joints and of marrow, and discerning the thoughts and intentions of the heart" (Hebrews 4:12). It is an incredible sword. It is sharp enough to fight off the enemy, and it is careful enough to be used as a scalpel on our own hearts.

Dear God, thank You for Your word. Help me to read it daily so that I can use it in my fight against sin. Amen.

Strong Men
Pray

⇒ Day 12 ⇐

The Priority of Prayer

> *"praying at all times in the Spirit,
> with all prayer and supplication."*
> EPHESIANS 6:18

After this call to stand firm and a breakdown of the armor of God, Paul gives the first command for the war-ready believer: pray. This seems and feels counterintuitive. As I read this passage, I thought, "Surely, he is going to encourage us to fight!" As I have thought about it, I've realized that is exactly what he has commanded us to do. Prayer is one of the greatest weapons against our enemy. It is the embodiment of being strong in the Lord!

We are wholly dependent on God in our fight against sin, temptation, and Satan. He has provided the armor necessary, the strength to stand, and he will provide by way of our prayers through every trial. Fight the natural urge to do it all by yourself. Rely fully on Jesus. Tell Him your struggles and ask Him for the ability to press on.

*Dear God, I give up fighting in my own strength.
I surrender my life to You. Teach me to pray
daily to You. Amen.*

Private Prayer

> ""And when you pray, you must not be like the hypocrites. For they love to stand and pray in the synagogues and at the street corners, that they may be seen by others. Truly, I say to you, they have received their reward. ⁶ But when you pray, go into your room and shut the door and pray to your Father who is in secret. And your Father who sees in secret will reward you."
> MATTHEW 6:5–6

Maybe you're reading this section about prayer and feeling overwhelmed or confused. Maybe you've never thought through the details of what a vibrant prayer life looks like. Maybe you don't feel like you know how to pray. You have a gracious Savior in Jesus who teaches His disciples to pray in Matthew 6.

The first thing he teaches is the concept of private prayer. He does not mean that you cannot pray in public or that no one should ever hear you pray. Throughout this sermon, Jesus uses hyperbole to emphasize His point. He is teaching that your prayers aren't primarily meant for men to hear but for God. So pray like it's just you and Him talking. Be honest with Him about your fears and joys in life.

Dear God, teach me to pray like nobody's watching. Captivate my heart as I bow my head to talk with you. Amen.

⇒ Day 14 ⇐
Thoughtful Prayer

> *"And when you pray, do not heap up empty phrases as the Gentiles do, for they think that they will be heard for their many words. 8 Do not be like them, for your Father knows what you need before you ask him."*
> MATTHEW 6:7-8

The next lesson on prayer from our Lord is about being thoughtful when we pray. The Gentiles he is referring to is anyone who is non-Jewish. That includes a wide variety of beliefs and prayer practices. Some belief systems teach that praying a certain mantra a certain number of times increases your chances of being heard by God. Within the Christian faith, it seems as if some believe that the more eloquent you are, the more God will listen to you. Jesus teaches us that neither of these things is true.

Your prayers to God are not meant to be rote repetition or impressive. Your prayers should be genuine, heartfelt, and honest. Sometimes your prayers will be all over the place. Sometimes you won't know a single word to say. Don't let that hinder you. God knows what you need before you even ask. He simply wants you to ask.

Dear God, I often don't have the right words to say. I trust that you understand my heart and hear me when I call. Amen.

God-Honoring Prayer

> *"Pray then like this: 'Our Father in heaven,*
> *hallowed be your name."*
> MATTHEW 6:9

Here we find the beginning of the Lord's prayer. This is not a special prayer that is particularly persuasive in the ears of God. This is a model prayer. Jesus is teaching us to pray about these things in these ways. We don't have to cover all of these bases with each and every prayer, but our prayer life as a whole should be marked by these things.

The first is that our prayer needs to be God-honoring. When we approach the throne of grace through prayer, we must recognize the glory of the One we're speaking to. We need to recognize His holiness and might. We need to remember his grace and mercy. We need to honor his name as we begin our conversation with the Most High God.

Dear God, You are worthy of all honor and praise.
I don't deserve the privilege of speaking to One so holy and
mighty. Thank You for listening to me, Your child. Amen.

Missional Prayer

> *"Your kingdom come, your will be done,*
> *on earth as it is in heaven."*
> MATTHEW 6:10

The second way that Jesus teaches us to pray is missional. Jesus' whole life was dedicated to doing the will of the Father. He preached that the kingdom of God was at hand, and so we must repent and believe. Jesus longed for the perfect reign of God, without any rebellion of sinful mankind, to be on earth as it is in heaven.

This should be our desire, as well. It is bigger than ourselves. It eclipses some of the smaller things that we worry about. It puts our plans into perspective. This line forces us to ask ourselves if we are concerned with the kingdom of God when we pray. Are we pursuing His perfect will as it is presented in Scripture or our own? Do you recognize His plans as more significant than your own?

Dear God, I confess that I am not always kingdom-minded. Convict me of these things, Father. Focus my eyes on Your goals. Amen.

Dependent Prayer

"Give us this day our daily bread,"
MATTHEW 6:11

I so appreciate this line in Jesus' prayer. Consider this thought, the Sustainer of all things (Colossians 1:17) is asking for daily sustenance. A thought that would never cross the mind of an All-powerful God has come to Jesus' mind because He took on human flesh for us. He humbled Himself to feel everything that we feel and need all that we need.

And like us, He confidently prayed to the Father to give Him all He needed, even daily bread. Jesus models for us what dependent prayer looks like. It's the prayer that swallows pride and self-righteousness and says, "Yes, God. I need You to provide for me." It is also a prayer that knows that God is a good Father. It trusts that He will not withhold from His children what they need.

Dear God, I trust you to provide for my needs. Even when I don't understand how or when, teach me to depend on You. Amen.

⇒ Day 18 ⇐

Merciful Prayer

> *"and forgive us our debts,*
> *as we also have forgiven our debtors."*
> MATTHEW 6:12

Once again, Jesus brings us back to the heart of the Gospel. Yes, we need daily bread. But what we need more urgently is forgiveness from our sins against God. Without this, we have no audience before the Father to hear our prayers in the first place.

Notice, though, that He doesn't only model asking for forgiveness. He models that we are going to need help forgiving others, as well. This is hard work! How quickly we can forget the mercy that was shown to us. Here Jesus shows us that our strength to forgive others is deeply rooted in our remembrance of the gospel. Therefore, as you embrace the mercy you receive from the Father, let that overflow into the relationships in your life.

Dear God, forgive me. I have sinned against you countless times. I thank You for Your faithful mercy. Help me show that mercy to others. Amen.

Righteous Prayer

"And lead us not into temptation,
but deliver us from evil."
MATTHEW 6:13

The final line in Jesus' model prayer should be regularly on our hearts. No matter how often we pray or how "good" we get at praying, we are all in danger of falling into temptation. We are sinfully and naturally bent to do just that. This is why we need the gracious help of our God to keep us from temptation.

Notice the second part of that sentence. Jesus knows that we will fall into temptation. This is why we need deliverance from the evil that follows it. As we have discussed, sin has heinous and damaging effects on our lives when we give in to it. It wields the weapon of death. Daily, we must rely on God to deliver us from that evil.

Dear God, you have been faithful to keep me from temptation and evil. I ask that you continue to guard my heart in this sinful world. Amen.

Prayer of Elijah

> *"Answer me, O Lord, answer me, that this people may know that you, O Lord, are God, and that you have turned their hearts back."*
> 1 KINGS 18:37

Standing on Mt. Carmel with hundreds of false prophets surrounding him, Elijah is alone. And yet, he has a smile on his face and confidence in his eyes. Elijah has challenged these false prophets to a contest between their gods. Both sides were to build an altar and place a sacrifice on it. Both sides were to pray to their god to accept the sacrifice by fire. The false prophets built their altar and prayed for hours on end and heard nothing but silence.

Elijah built his altar and doused it with water making it all the more difficult to light. Then he prayed. His prayer was righteous and compassionate. In essence, he prayed for a fire to be lit on the altar and in their hearts. His desire was not to be right but to be righteous. Let our prayers be categorized this way, as well.

Dear God, I call to you in prayer for many reasons, some selfish and some not. Would You help me to pray righteous prayers that have a concern for others and for Your glory? Amen.

Prayer of Jonah

> *"I called out to the Lord, out of my distress,
> and he answered me; out of the belly of Sheol I cried,
> and you heard my voice.."*
> JONAH 2:1

After being thrown overboard for his disobedience to God in the belly of a large fish, Jonah prayed. The story of Jonah is one of rebellion and selfishness on Jonah's part and great kindness on God's part. When Jonah fled from his commission to preach to Nineveh, God could have let him go. God could have killed him. But no, God saved him, preserved him, and used him.

This prayer comes from the depths of the sea amid distress that Jonah brought on himself. But because Jonah knows he is dealing with a kind, merciful God, he could call out to him and know that he would hear and answer his voice. Maybe you're like Jonah today. You've been rebelling and are in trouble because of your actions. Cry out to God. He will hear you and answer you.

Dear God, I need help. I've made mistakes that have brought me to tears. Hear my prayer, O God. Amen.

Prayer of Solomon

"Give your servant therefore an understanding mind to govern your people, that I may discern between good and evil, for who is able to govern this your great people?"
1 KINGS 3:9

King Solomon was given the opportunity to ask God for anything. If I were him, I would have been tempted to ask for riches, health, prominence, or any other thing my selfish heart could imagine. But Solomon handles this situation differently. He asks God for wisdom. God grants him that request and supplies riches, health, and prominence as well.

Solomon prayed in such a way that he said, God, I want to do what you've called me to do well. I want to be a good king, so I need to be a wise king. God, desiring to see His people serve and glorify Him, gave him wisdom. We can confidently pray for wisdom too. James 1:5 teaches us that if anyone lacks wisdom, He can ask God for it, and God will give it freely.

Dear God, You know all things. There is nothing that You're unaware of. Give me wisdom so I may serve You better. Amen.

Prayer of David

> *"Therefore David inquired of the Lord, "Shall I go and attack these Philistines?" And the Lord said to David, "Go and attack the Philistines and save Keilah.""*
> 1 SAMUEL 23:2

Have you ever had to make a life-altering decision and had no idea what to do? That's where David is in this situation. He is working his way through a series of battles to lead God's people. Instead of only consulting his lead battle strategist, he consults God. He asks Him for clear direction on when and where to attack.

We, too, can go to God to ask Him what we should do when life is challenging. This Scripture doesn't teach that God will answer us in an audible voice every time, but it does show us that God answers His people. He may answer you through a trusted friend or life circumstances. However, God has spoken and speaks most clearly through His word. Pray to God and listen to what He says in the Bible.

Dear God, I don't know where to go or what to do. I need clear direction from you. Would you make your plans for me obvious? Amen.

Jesus Prays for You

"I am praying for them. I am not praying for the world but for those whom you have given me, for they are yours."
JOHN 17:9

In this passage of Scripture that we're about to walk through, we find an incredible truth. Jesus prays for you. He prays for all of His disciples and for their good. It is meaningful to know that someone is praying for you. Oftentimes we will even encourage others with the same sentiment. But, friends, it is a far greater encouragement and comfort to know that our Savior prayed over us, His people.

When you're feeling alone and discouraged, remember this sweet truth: Jesus prayed for you. Not only did He pray for you then, but He is also still interceding on your behalf before the Father (Romans 8:34). Jesus is still praying for you! His eyes and mind are on His people. He will not forget you.

Dear God, thank You for Your Son, who is interceding on my behalf as we speak. What an incredible thing that You would think of me so often. Amen.

Jesus Prays for You - Keep Them

> *"While I was with them, I kept them in your name, which you have given me. I have guarded them, and not one of them has been lost except the son of destruction, that the Scripture might be fulfilled."*
> JOHN 17:12

Jesus prays for specific things to be true of us as believers. The first is that we would be kept in His name. He knew that the disciples He was with were about to go through tumultuous times. They would see Him arrested, beaten, mocked, and finally crucified. They would see Him raised from the dead and share a meal with Him. Then they would see Him ascend to the Father as the Church would be born. They would face persecution of many kinds.

We will face persecution and temptation in our lives as well. It is Jesus' desire that we will be kept in His name. He wants us to always wear His jersey with pride, even if it feels like we're getting beat in the game of life. We need the strength of God to hold our heads up and be kept in His name.

Dear God, keep me in Your name. Don't let me stray to the left or the right. Give me Your strength, I pray. Amen.

43

Jesus Prays for You - Give Them Joy

> *"But now I am coming to you, and these things I speak in the world, that they may have my joy fulfilled in themselves."*
> JOHN 17:13

Jesus' prayer for us is for our joy. We would be crushed without it. If there wasn't joy at the end of the Christian life, the hardships, the denying of oneself, the difficult choices would feel pointless. But there is a great joy for us as we labor along in life. One day we will get to rejoice in the presence of our Savior! His kingdom will be one without sin, tears, or strife.

Jesus Himself held on to joy as He went to the cross. He was able to endure these things for the joy set before Him (Hebrews 12:2). What was that joy? The joy of glorifying the Father. The joy of saving His people. The joy of finishing the work He set out to do. We have a joy set before us as well. Let's run the race with endurance.

Dear God, what joy there is to be found in You, God. Allow me to experience this joy day to day. Amen.

⇒Day 27⇐

Jesus Prays for You - Protect Them

> *"I do not ask that you take them out of the world, but that you keep them from the evil one."*
> JOHN 17:15

There is great intentionality in this line of Jesus' prayer. He doesn't wish for us to leave the world and join Him in heaven right now. There is work still to be done. There are people who need to be saved. There are souls that need to be restored. We can't leave yet. Jesus, knowing this, prays that we would be protected from Satan, the evil one.

This brings back to mind what Paul taught about our enemy. It's not ultimately one of flesh and bones. Jesus Himself knew the physical dangers the disciples would face. Most of them would be martyred for their faith. His prayer was that they would be kept spiritually safe from the evil one. This is the kind of care your God has for you.

Dear God, the devil prowls like a lion. I am often scared and ready to be home with you. Keep me safe as I continue Your work. Amen.

Jesus Prays for You - Sanctify Them

> *"Sanctify them in the truth; your word is truth."*
> JOHN 17:17

Jesus prays for our sanctification. To be sanctified means to be set apart or different. Like a black sheep or a four-leaf clover, we should stand out. Jesus wants us to be in the world (as we learned before), but not of the world. We shouldn't look like everyone else around us.

How then should we live? What does it look like to live a sanctified life? We must live in light of God's word. We are sanctified by the truth, and God's word is truth. This means we won't always physically look different from the world. We will, however, have different ideals, goals, and worldviews. It makes the disposition of our souls and hearts different from those in the world who are not believers.

Dear God, I need Your word to sanctify me.
Help me to be a man of Your word. Amen.

⇒Day 29⇐

Jesus Prays for You - Unify Them

> *"I in them and you in me, that they may become perfectly one, so that the world may know that you sent me and loved them even as you loved me."*
> JOHN 17:23

"If a house is divided against itself, it cannot stand" (Mark 3:25). This principle of unity that Jesus taught to His disciples and rebuked the Pharisees with is the same principle that He prays will be found in us. Notice the depth of unity He prays for. He desires that our unity would mirror the unity of the Father and the Son. This is a perfect relationship of love and respect for one another.

This the type of unity we must strive for among ourselves as believers. It is far too easy for us to break fellowship over various points of theology, traditions, or cultural values. We must persevere in the fight for unity. It is the prayer of Christ and our great witness to a watching, divided world.

Dear God, I don't always agree with my brother or sister in Christ. And if I'm honest, I don't always like them. Help me to pursue unity in your gospel above all else. Amen.

47

Jesus Prays for You - Be With Them

> *"Father, I desire that they also, whom you have given me, may be with me where I am, to see my glory that you have given me because you loved me before the foundation of the world."*
> JOHN 17:24

From Genesis to Revelation, we see Gods' desire to be with His people. This is a mind-boggling truth at times. We are rebellious, spiteful, and arrogant people. If I were Him, I wouldn't want to be with me! And yet, He pursues relationships with His people time and time again.

Here we find Jesus voicing that prayer to the Father. He wants to be with His people. In some sense, He will miss them as He is away from them in heaven. He desires, even now, to have them in His presence so they can see His glory. Brother, He desires to be with you, and one day He will make that happen.

Dear God, I want to be with you. I want to see Your glory. I want to know you. Amen.

Jesus Prays for You - Love Them

> *"I made known to them your name, and I will continue to make it known, that the love with which you have loved me may be in them, and I in them."*
> JOHN 17:26

The Father loves the Son in a perfect, selfless, beautiful way that we cannot fully understand and have yet to experience. It is deeper than the love of a father and more faithful than the love of a husband. It encompasses all the qualities found in 1 Corinthians 13.

This is the love that Jesus prays we will receive from the Father. Not a watered-down version or even an equal percentage of love, but the full, everlasting love of an Almighty God. Jesus loves you and wants you to be loved immensely. This changes how we view God, ourselves, and others. In light of God's unrelenting love, we can live lives that are for Him and His glory.

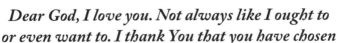

Dear God, I love you. Not always like I ought to or even want to. I thank You that you have chosen to love me always. Amen.

Praying for Others

> *"We ought always to give thanks to God for you, brothers, as is right, because your faith is growing abundantly, and the love of every one of you for one another is increasing."*
> 2 THESSALONIANS 1:3

Paul tells the churches that he is involved in how he prays for them. Paul is someone who consistently prays for other people. The thing he says most often is how he thanks God for those who are in his life. He is thankful to know them, watch them grow, and even struggle with them.

Do you thank God for the people in your life? He has surrounded you with friends, family, co-workers, or all of the above. You get the privilege of being involved in the lives of others and making an impact. Take time to thank God for those people who are in your life that are special to you. He has given them to you as a good gift from a loving father.

Dear God, thank you for all of the special people in my life. Use me to encourage and love them every day. Amen.

Praying for Others' Love

"and may the Lord make you increase and abound in love for one another and for all, as we do for you, "
1 THESSALONIANS 3:12

Jesus taught that people will know we are His disciples based on how we love one another. So it is fitting that this is one of Paul's prayers for his brothers and sisters in Christ at the church in Thessalonica. He prays that their love not only increases but abounds as well. Like filling up a glass with water, he wants it to overflow.

We ought to pray for this kind of love for others as well. This would be incredibly helpful as we consider those with whom we don't have a good relationship. A love for others is a product of the gospel. Because Jesus has loved us in our sin, then we must strive to love others who may sin against us.

Dear God, I pray for my friends, family, and enemies. Increase the love in their lives. Help them to love one another as You have loved them. Amen.

⇒Day 34⇐
Praying for Others' Holiness

> "so that he may establish your hearts blameless in holiness before our God and Father, at the coming of our Lord Jesus with all his saints."
> 1 THESSALONIANS 3:13

Depending on how you read this, you may get the wrong impression of Paul. This is not him looking down on the Thessalonian church with a holier-than-thou attitude. This is a genuine prayer from a concerned and loving pastor. At his core, that is who Paul was in his ministry; a church planter and pastor. He does not want to see his friends grow stagnant or fall back in their faith.

Do you have this kind of concern for those around you? Do you rejoice at their progress in the faith? I challenge you to pray for the holiness of others. Don't pray in an arrogant or prideful way, but compassionately and encouragingly. Let them know that you're genuinely praying for them as well and see that it will spur them on to continue to grow.

Dear God, help me to look at my friends with care for their souls in mind. Use me to spur them on towards holiness. Amen.

Strong Men

Battle

We Lost the Battle

> *"So when the woman saw that the tree was good for food, and that it was a delight to the eyes, and that the tree was to be desired to make one wise, she took of its fruit and ate, and she also gave some to her husband who was with her, and he ate"*
> GENESIS 3:6

Before we begin this conversation on how strong men battle sin, we must acknowledge that we lost in the beginning. In a good world, Adam and Eve chose to disobey God's word. They believed the lie of Satan and sinned against God. The fact of the matter is, whether it was Adam and Eve or you and me, we all have sinned against God. We have all lost the battle. Ephesians 2:3 tells us that sinfulness is in our very nature.

This seems to leave little hope for us to fight. It feels like we're up against Goliath. In our own strength, we are. But like David, we are confident that we fight our battles "in the strength of His might." So, let's wage war against temptation and the sins that seek us out.

Dear God, if it were up to me, I would lose every fight against temptation. I need Your strength, and I trust that You will supply it. Amen.

In Christ, We Win the War

> *"For as by the one man's disobedience the many were made sinners, so by the one man's obedience the many will be made righteous."*
> ROMANS 5:19

Although we have lost the battle originally, Jesus has won the war! Through "one man's" (Adam's) disobedience, we are all stained with sin. But through "one man's" (Jesus') obedience, we are all provided the opportunity of righteousness. This is the good news of the gospel for us. God did not leave us to die in our sin. He sent a better Adam!

We will lose many battles in our war against sin. We will lash out in anger. We will give into that addiction. We will be selfish and lazy. We will lose time and time again. But in Christ, we have won the war! Through His victory, we can be hopeful and find joy. We can win our daily battles with sin because of the victory He has won for us. All is not lost!

Dear God, I am so thankful for Your Son, the better Adam. Thank You for sending Him to do what I cannot do and live the life I cannot live. Amen.

Daily Battle

> " *For I do not do the good I want, but the evil I do not want is what I keep on doing.* "
> ROMANS 7:19

With Adam's original sin tainting us all and Jesus' sacrifice giving us salvation, we are in between two worlds. We still wrestle with our sin every day even though Jesus has given us the victory. We haven't fully experienced the freedom that our salvation brings. We won't experience that until we are with Him in heaven or He comes back again.

Until then, we will be like Paul. There will be days where we do what we don't want to do, and we don't do what we do want to do. There is a battle for our souls each and every day. In one corner stands our sinful flesh, and in the other, the Holy Spirit. If we fight in the strength that God provides, He will work through us and give us victory.

Dear God, there is a battle raging inside of me.
I pray that You will help me in the fight. Amen.

Battle Strategy from Joseph - Refuse

" But he refused and said to his master's wife . . ."
GENESIS 39:8

The book of Genesis gives us the story of Joseph. His story is incredible and filled with deep love, betrayal, and great forgiveness. Joseph provides us with a great example of what it looks like to fight sin during his crazy life story. Over the next few days, we will take a look at this example in detail.

While working for his master, Joseph was tempted by his master's wife to sleep with her. From the very first temptation, Joseph refused her. This is step one for us. The moment the temptation comes, we must refuse. We cannot think about it for a while and allow it to persuade us. The longer we entertain the thought, the harder it will be to refuse it in the end.

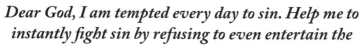

Dear God, I am tempted every day to sin. Help me to instantly fight sin by refusing to even entertain the thought of it. Amen.

57

Battle Strategy from Joseph - Ripple Effect

> *"Behold, because of me my master has no concern about anything in the house, and he has put everything that he has in my charge."*
> GENESIS 39:8

After Joseph refused his master's wife, he explained part of his reasoning. I want us to take note of that. He says that he cannot sleep with her because his master has been nothing but good. His master has trusted him with everything in his house, including his wife. Sinning in this way would not only be hurtful to Joseph but to his master and his master's wife.

Our sins have residual effects. While we may sin in isolation or just with one other person, there are always ripple effects. Sin hardens your heart and closes you off to those around you. Also, when your sin comes to light, the damage of deception is difficult to reconcile. The next time you're tempted, remember sin is never harmless.

Dear God, remind me of the evil of my sin. Remind me how destructive it is and use that to drive me away from it. Amen.

Battle Strategy from Joseph - Ultimate Offense

> *"He is not greater in this house than I am, nor has he kept back anything from me except you, because you are his wife. How then can I do this great wickedness and sin against God?"*
> **GENESIS 39:9**

Here Joseph continues to explain his refusal to his master's wife. Not only would it be sinning against him, but it would also be sinning against God. What a terrifying thought: that we would sin against our Creator. He alone is the one who can destroy both body and soul (Matthew 10:28)

How is this a sin against God? She is not God's wife, is she? How is this "great wickedness and sin against God?" Any time that we break the law of God, we sin against Him. It is God who said, "Do not commit adultery." While those sins involve other people, and we are sinning against them, we are also sinning directly against God. This shows us the sticky and destructive effects of sin. The cracks it causes go deeper and deeper.

Dear God, I confess to You that all of my sins are ultimately against You. I stand accused, but by Your grace, I do not stand condemned. Amen.

Battle Strategy from Joseph - Persistence

> *"And as she spoke to Joseph day after day, he would not listen to her, to lie beside her or to be with her."*
> GENESIS 39:10

What Joseph experiences here, we can all relate to. Just because you're successful in refusing temptation one time does not mean that it will go away. It does not mean that it will even leave you alone for a little while before it comes back. The Bible says that she tempted Joseph "day after day." As we can imagine, this temptation got stronger and more alluring as time went on.

Notice how Joseph responds to this temptation. It says that "he would not listen to her." Each and every day, he continued to do what he did in the beginning. He refused to even listen to her. The truth is that Joseph was a real man and his master's wife was very beautiful. The temptation was there, and it was strong. So Joseph did not give Satan a foothold. He refused to even listen to the temptation.

———⦾———

Dear God, would you give me the discipline to not even listen to the temptation. The moment it comes my way, help me to shut it down. Amen.

———⦾———

Battle Strategy from Joseph - Run

> *"But he left his garment in her hand and fled and got out of the house."*
> GENESIS 39:12

When temptation is persistent and refusal to listen still isn't working, Joseph shows us the next step. This is the next plan of attack for the believer. The temptation was growing stronger and more aggressive. So aggressive that when Joseph ran away, she tore the clothes right off of him. So Joseph made a bold move. He ran. He literally ran away from the temptation.

Brother, this is not too drastic a move for us to make. There are going to be times when you need to literally flee from temptation. If you're in a situation where temptation is strong, and you feel like you won't be able to resist, run. Leave the room. Take a walk. Get in your car and drive away. We do not always have to run, but when refusal doesn't work, run with the strength that the Lord provides.

Dear God, teach me to run. Help me be aware of when I'm in over my head, and I just need to flee. Amen.

Battle Strategy from Joseph - Trust

> *"But the Lord was with Joseph and showed him steadfast love and gave him favor in the sight of the keeper of the prison."*
> GENESIS 39:21

This is the final thing I want to note about Joseph's fight against sin in Scripture. The life he lived was overflowing with the "steadfast love" of God. Ultimately, it is God who kept him from falling into temptation. When Joseph overcame sin by God's grace, he was protected by the Father.

Because his master believed the lies of his wife, Joseph was thrown into prison. God did not leave him to rot in jail, nor did He reward his faithfulness with punishment. God used the painful outcome of his circumstances to move Joseph on his journey that saved his family. When we're fighting hard against sin, and it seems like our lives are not getting any easier, remember that you're still covered in the love of God. You may feel like you're sitting in a prison cell that you don't deserve. Trust that God has a plan in store for you. Keep up the fight.

Dear God, this life is a battle sometimes. There are many times when I feel like I've been dealt a bad hand. Help me to trust You through it all. Amen.

Wisdom for the War - Do Not Consent

> *"My son, if sinners entice you, do not consent."*
> PROVERBS 1:10

Lessons on how to battle against temptation come from the stories we read in the Bible and the wisdom literature that we find. Solomon, the king who prayed for wisdom, wrote Proverbs' book, and we are still gleaning from his holy advice today.

The first piece of advice we are given is to not consent to sinners. To consent means to "give permission for something to happen." The implication for us here is that we have the power in the situation. As blood-bought people of God, we do not have to sin. We have a choice to make. We can choose to continue to walk in life or dabble in the damaging effect of death-causing sin. Brother, do not consent.

Dear God, as Your people, we are in a new position. Before Christ, I had no power to fight against temptation, but now You've given me the strength. Help me to not give in. Amen.

Wisdom for the War - Avoid the Path

> *"Do not enter the path of the wicked, and do not walk in the way of the evil. Avoid it; do not go on it; turn away from it and pass on."*
> PROVERBS 4:14-15

Don't go there. Usually, when we hear this phrase, it's about a subject we better not broach. But here, Solomon is teaching us to not go towards sinful situations. If you struggle with the misuse of alcohol, don't go to a bar. If you struggle with pornography, don't be on your phone or computer alone at night. If you struggle with pride, don't spend all your free time on social media comparing your life to another's.

We all have sinful bents and habits that we are fighting against. One of the best strategies against those temptations is not putting ourselves in that position to begin with. Instead of going towards sin, walk in righteousness (Psalm 1). Don't go there.

Dear God, give me the wisdom to stay away from tempting situations. I trust that You will keep me from falling. Amen.

Wisdom for the War - Be Aware

> *"For the lips of a forbidden woman drip honey, and her speech is smoother than oil, but in the end she is bitter as wormwood, sharp as a two-edged sword."*
> PROVERBS 5:3-4

Solomon here gives us a picture of what temptation is like. It is alluring and enticing. It sells itself as something sweet and satisfying. It promises joy and happiness with its indulgence, but Solomon gives us the full picture. When we bite into the temptation, we will always find it to be bitter and painful.

Let's be aware that sin is truly tempting. If it didn't look pleasurable and offer us these promises of happiness, why would we sin, to begin with? Our foe has laced these temptations with poison. He is out to deceive his enemies. Don't believe the lies. Don't take the fruit. It will always end in bitterness and hurt.

Dear God, I confess that sin looks so good. It can feel so right. Help me to see past the proposed sweetness and taste in advance the bitterness to come. Amen.

Wisdom for the War - Flee Sinful Situations

"Let your fountain be blessed, and rejoice in the wife of your youth, like a lovely deer, a graceful doe. Let her breasts fill you at all times with delight; be intoxicated always in her love."

PROVERBS 5:18-19

Once again, Solomon puts in our mind a portrait of righteousness. Not only are we to flee temptation and refuse sinful thoughts, but we are to replace them with holy meditation and run towards godliness. Where we are tempted towards adultery, Solomon says, run toward your wife. Enjoy the good gift that God has given you. Let your temptation be overshadowed by the joy of obedience to the Father.

This is not just applicable in marriage relationships. If you're tempted towards gossip, share the gospel instead. If you're tempted towards anger, put that energy towards weight lifting. If you're tempted towards slothfulness, find something productive that you truly enjoy doing. Let's not just run from sin. Let's run towards holiness.

Dear God, I want to flee sinful situations. I don't always know which way to go. Make it clear to me what a holy alternative to that temptation would be. Amen.

Wisdom for the War - Desire the Right Things

> *"Do not desire her beauty in your heart, and do not let her capture you with her eyelashes;"*
> PROVERBS 6:25

The heart of the matter is the matter of the heart. We can practice all the things that we have seen in Joseph's life and all the advice we have gleaned from Solomon and still fall short of our goal. At the end of the day, running away will only get you so far. Diving into a "good" thing to avoid a bad thing will only last so long. The issue at hand is a heart issue.

This is why Solomon tells us not to desire the beauty of sin in our hearts lest we be captured. The condition of our hearts is not something we can fix on our own. We cannot make our hearts good or holy. Only God can give us new hearts. This is why we need Jesus so desperately in the fight. He alone can give us what we need.

Dear God, my heart is sinful and in desperate need of replacement. Give me a new heart through the work of Christ. Amen.

Wisdom for the War - Store the Word

> *"I have stored up your word in my heart,*
> *that I might not sin against you."*
> PSALM 119:11

O nce we have a new heart given to us by God, how can we keep it pure? How can we prevent disease? Psalm 119 gives us the medicine we need: the word of God. Notice that it is not just reading the word or doing a devotional study that protects our hearts. It is the act of storing God's word in our hearts that does the work.

It's like charging your phone. If we're careful, we can go a day or two without recharging it, but we will see the effects. It will begin to slow down. We will have to use it less often. Eventually, it will just die. Storing God's word in our heart is like recharging your heart. You need it daily and plugging in for a minute does little good.

⎯⎯⎯⎯⎯⎯⎯ ∽◯∾ ⎯⎯⎯⎯⎯⎯⎯

Dear God, help me to store Your word in my heart so that I will not sin against You. Amen.

⎯⎯⎯⎯⎯⎯⎯ ∽◯∾ ⎯⎯⎯⎯⎯⎯⎯

Battle Scars - Ensnared

> *"The iniquities of the wicked ensnare him, and he is held fast in the cords of his sin."*
> PROVERBS 5:22

The reality of sin is that we will all succumb to it at different points in our lives. And sin will always leave scars behind. To encourage us to keep from sinning, let's look at the different wounds that it can cause.

The first is that sin traps and binds us. We have all experienced this in different ways. Maybe you have dealt with the more severe form of this in addition, or maybe you've only felt yourself caught in a web of lies. My dad used to say this to me: "Oh, what a tangled web we weave when at first we choose to deceive." Sin will bind us the longer we toy with it. Like a fish caught in a net, we don't realize it until it is too late.

Dear God, I have been ensnared by sins that I am ashamed of. Set me free to live for your glory. Amen.

Battle Scars - Death

> *"For the wages of sin is death . . ."*
> ROMANS 6:23

Sin brings with it the ultimate scar: death. No matter the sin, whether a little lie or a heinous murder, all sin brings the same ultimate price tag. This is not a direct reference to physical death. It is talking about spiritual death. Our sins kill our souls and damage our relationship with God.

Perhaps we ought to spend more time counting the cost of our sin. If we view the collateral damage for our sinful choices in eternal and spiritual terms, we will be more mindful of what we're doing rather than temporal and physical. The double-take at the beautiful woman passing by might actually be us staring into the face of death.

Dear God, sin brings a price that I cannot pay.
I praise You that You have paid it all by
the sacrifice of Your Son. Amen.

⇒Day 52⇐
Battle Scars - Separation

> *"but your iniquities have made a separation between you and your God, and your sins have hidden his face from you so that he does not hear."*
> ISAIAH 59:2

As I write this devotional, there is a global pandemic requiring us to keep physical distance from one another. This has forced loved ones to spend time apart and even miss major life events that would have normally brought so much joy. In many cases, there is a shield of plexiglass between another person and us.

Sin has this effect on our relationship with God. It separates us from Him. But unlike plexiglass, it hides us from Him. It's like a wall that is being built between us. Christ has broken that wall down for us, but we often like to put a few bricks back up and indulge in old sinful habits. Know that this is damaging our relationship with our Savior, the One who broke down the wall for us.

Dear God, forgive me for trying to build back the wall that You have broken down. Amen.

⇒ Day 53 ⇐

Battle Scars - Find You Out

> *"But if you will not do so, behold, you have sinned against the Lord, and be sure your sin will find you out."*
> NUMBERS 32:23

Sin does not stay hidden forever. Some of us have become experts at hiding our sins away from others. We stash receipts, delete our browsing history, say that a meeting ran long at work, whatever it takes to keep others from finding out our secrets.

This is a vain mission. The Bible makes it clear that our sins will come to light. Many of us have experienced this in some way or another. Others have seen the skeletons in the closet of someone who passed away. One way or another, the truth will come to light. And when it does, we will all need forgiveness. Sin offers no protection. It will leave you high and dry. Instead of waiting for that terrible day, confess your sins to God and be met with mercy and forgiveness.

Dear God, I am tired of hiding. I know confessing my sins will have consequences, but I trust that the sweetness of mercy and forgiveness will overshadow it all. Amen.

Balm for a Wounded Soul - No Condemnation

> *"There is therefore now no condemnation for those who are in Christ Jesus."*
> ROMANS 8:1

If you're feeling discouraged and beaten, hold on just a little bit longer. While many scars accompany our sins, there is a balm for our wounded souls all the more. Let's take a few days to enjoy this good news.

The Bible says that if we are in Christ, meaning that we have trusted Him as our savior, then there is no condemnation for us. That means that, although we have earned the punishment of death and eternity in Hell, we are not condemned to those punishments. Jesus has taken the full wrath of God for our sins on Himself. What a glorious truth that we get to walk in as His people.

Dear God, I feel condemned, but I am not. I stand forgiven by You because of the life, death, and resurrection of Your Son. Thank You. Amen.

Balm for a Wounded Soul - An Advocate

> *"My little children, I am writing these things to you so that you may not sin. But if anyone does sin, we have an advocate with the Father, Jesus Christ the righteous."*
> 1 JOHN 2:1

Jesus not only saves us from condemnation, but He is also our advocate with the Father. He fights on our behalf. He makes sure that the Father replaces our record of wrong with His record of perfection. He reminds Him that we are forgiven due to His work. He stands in our place and pleads our case.

There is great security in Jesus. He didn't save us so that we could try again and try not to fail. He saved us and kept us in His salvation. Every time we fall short, He is there to pick us back up. Until we are in Heaven with God or Jesus returns, we can be confident of two things: we will continue to struggle with sin, and Jesus will continue to defend us.

Dear God, what good news we have as Your Children! Jesus has saved us and keeps us in Your love by His gracious work for us. Amen.

Balm for a Wounded Soul - Jesus Keeps Us

"Now to him who is able to keep you from stumbling and to present you blameless before the presence of his glory with great joy,"
JUDE 1:24

This verse takes us all the way back to the title of this book. It's a tangible example of what it means to be strong in the Lord and in the strength of His might. Jude teaches us here that it is Jesus who can keep us from stumbling and present us blameless. I want you to see the pervasiveness of the gospel in our lives.

Jesus saves us. Jesus advocates for us. Jesus keeps us from even stumbling in the first place. Every victory that we have is because of Jesus. Every success in fleeing temptation is due to His strength and not our own. We owe everything we have to Him. This beautiful truth should drive us towards deeper dependence on Him.

Dear God, I so desperately need you if I'm going to fight these battles. You can provide all that I need. Amen.

Balm for a Wounded Soul - An Escape

"No temptation has overtaken you that is not common to man. God is faithful, and he will not let you be tempted beyond your ability, but with the temptation he will also provide the way of escape, that you may be able to endure it."
1 CORINTHIANS 10:13

There is a lot of sweet truth in this verse. The first is that you're not alone in the temptation that you're facing. Anything that you're being tempted with is "common to man." The devil tries to convince you that you're the only one dealing with this and that others will reject you if you tell them about it. Don't believe the lie. You're not alone!

The second is that God will always provide a way of escape from every temptation. There is always an opportunity to flee. The difficulty lies in identifying those opportunities and acting on them. This is where we once again need God's help in our lives.

Dear God, thank You for the encouragement that I am not alone and not without an escape. Help me to see the escape from temptation that You provide every time. Amen.

Balm for a Wounded Soul - Sympathetic High Priest

"For we do not have a high priest who is unable to sympathize with our weaknesses, but one who in every respect has been tempted as we are, yet without sin."
HEBREWS 4:15

This might be the most comforting verse in our fight against sin. We learned in the last passage that we are not alone. Other people have been through the temptations that you're facing. This verse teaches us that Jesus Himself has had to fight the temptations that you're fighting.

Not only has He fought them, but He has been victorious in every instance. This is the strong God that we worship. This is the mighty God that has saved us. He has proven Himself to be able to handle anything that life can throw at us. He has endured it, and He was won. It is in His strength that we have the joy of continuing in the fight.

Dear God, You are mighty, and You are victorious! There is no temptation in my life that You cannot handle. I trust You. Amen.

How Jesus Fought - The Word of God

> *"And Jesus answered him, "It is written,*
> *'Man shall not live by bread alone."*
> LUKE 4:4

Finally, in this section on the fight that we face, let's examine how Jesus fought against temptation. As we have already seen, he was fully successful in every battle. So, what did He do to ward off the enticement of Satan?

While in the wilderness, Satan came to Jesus to personally tempt Him face to face. Jesus responds every time with the Word of God. He refutes the lies of the devil with the reliable truth of God's word. This is how we must fight as well. When the devil tempts us to believe that God is withholding some kind of good or that there is a greater joy for us in other things, we must respond to him with the facts that God's word offers us.

Dear God, there are convincing lies that are being told to me by my flesh, the world, and the devil. Remind me of Your truth. Amen.

How Jesus Fought - Know Your Lord

"And Jesus answered him, "It is written, ""You shall worship the Lord your God, and him only shall you serve.""
LUKE 4:8

Not only did Jesus respond with the Word of God at every enticement, but He also reminded Himself and the devil who it is that He serves. This can be an invaluable thing for us to do. We have a natural desire to serve ourselves. We want to be our own God. Satan knows that about us and wants to play into that. He wants to convince us that we need or deserve something that doesn't belong to us.

We need to do whatever it takes to remind ourselves of who we worship and serve. Whether we quote Scripture when temptation comes, sing a worship song, or pause and pray, we must keep our minds focused on the One we serve.

Dear God, You alone are my King. I worship and serve You, for You are gracious and kind. Amen.

How Jesus Fought - Rely on the Word

> *"And Jesus answered him, "It is said, 'You shall not put the Lord your God to the test.'"*
> LUKE 4:12

The final temptation that Satan had for Jesus was as tricky as they come. He challenged the strength of God and quoted Scripture to support his statements. He used the tactic of Jesus' defense against Him. Satan was only doing what he always does. He was twisting the truth into a lie. Jesus did not take the bait. He didn't puff out His chest and say, "watch this." He refused to play the game the devil was trying to play.

Just as Satan did what he always did, Jesus did what He always did: He relied on the Word of God. Instead of twisting it to say what He wanted to say, Jesus simply let the Word of God speak for itself. Satan is crafty and will try everything he can to get you to fall. Don't let go of the sure Word of God.

Dear God, help me to fight temptation like Jesus. Teach me to rely on Your word at all times. Amen.

The Battle Continues

> *"And when the devil had ended every temptation, he departed from him until an opportune time."*
> LUKE 4:13

Even after the devil had lost in a tremendous display of the steadfastness of Jesus, he didn't give up. He left until an opportune time presented itself. He laid in wait, looking for the best possible time to trip Jesus up and cause Him to sin. This is the devil that is stalking you. He is persistent and cunning. He is waiting for the opportune time to attack.

Don't let that cause you grief or worry, friend. For Satan was never successful in his attacks against our savior. Even after leading men to have Him crucified, he still was not the victor. He cannot overcome or defeat Jesus. If we are in Christ, we have nothing to fear. Let the war rage on. We know the Conquering King.

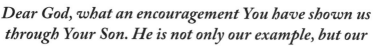

Dear God, what an encouragement You have shown us through Your Son. He is not only our example, but our strength to follow suit. Amen.

Strong Men

Study

Psalm 119 - Blessed Life

> *"Blessed are those who keep his testimonies, who seek him with their whole heart,"*
> PSALM 119:2

When we think of strength, we don't often think of someone reading a book. We think of someone in the weight room or on the battlefield. But as we will see and have seen so far, the strong man of God holds tightly to the word of God. It is the man who sets aside time to read the Bible regularly.

Psalm 119 is the longest and is an in-depth reflection on the necessity of God's word. Over the next few days, we will take time to study select verses from it. I would recommend reading a section or two of the psalm each day as we walk through this together. Doing this will lead us in the way of the blessed life, as this verse teaches. In other words, it will lead to an inner strength that provides peace and joy in all seasons of life.

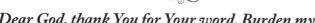

Dear God, thank You for Your word. Burden my heart to read it every day and look to You for the blessing. Amen.

Psalm 119 - Pure Way

> *"How can a young man keep his way pure?*
> *By guarding it according to your word."*
> PSALM 119:9

We cannot all classify ourselves as young men anymore, but this verse's core truth remains. We can raise our defenses by burying our minds and hearts in the word of God. Having a heart devoted to the word is less like a horse with blinders and more like a soldier with night-vision goggles.

It doesn't work for the Christian to spend all his energies trying to block out anything tempting. What the believer needs is a more discerning heart. He needs to be able to look out into the darkness and navigate this life. Let's keep our way pure by devoting ourselves to taking in God's word. Let it wash over the eyes of our hearts and color the way we see the world around us.

Dear God, keep me in Your word and keep
me by Your word, I pray. Amen.

Psalm 119 - Open My Eyes

"Open my eyes, that I may behold wondrous things out of your law."
PSALM 119:18

Let's be honest. Sometimes reading the Bible can be challenging, discouraging, and (dare I say it) boring. There are mile-long lists of names and numbers about people and places that we don't always understand. When we're facing seasons like this, Psalm 119:18 is a great prayer to practice.

It confesses that our eyes are closed to the significance of the Bible sometimes. Even though we may have read it over and over, we still may not get it. It also trusts there are wondrous things to behold in each passage of Scripture, even the mundane and monotonous portions. If you're stuck, pray and press on. Don't let the frustration or discouragement keep you from the incredible truths the Bible has to offer.

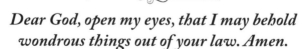

Dear God, open my eyes, that I may behold wondrous things out of your law. Amen.

Psalm 119 - Crushed Soul

"My soul is consumed with longing for your rules at all times."
PSALM 119:20

Here the Psalmist describes a heart-posture as he goes throughout his life. It's an intense one and hyperbolic to prove a point. He is not grief-stricken and unable to do anything else in his life. However, in comparison to the other things vying for his attention, his soul is utterly captivated by the word of God.

What a challenging concept for us to consider! We have so many things pulling us in all kinds of directions. Perhaps you've already been pulled away by a text message or notification while reading this devotional. Take time to think and ask yourself, could I say that my soul is consumed with longing for the Scripture? If not, then why? What priorities do I need to reconsider this week?

Dear God, give me a deep, strong desire to know and study Your word. I confess I have been pulled away from it too often. Amen.

Psalm 119 - Give Me Life

> *"My soul clings to the dust; give me life according to your word!"*
> PSALM 119:25

Have you been there? Have you felt so beaten down and crushed by life that you feel like your soul is clinging on for dear life? Maybe you've experienced this pain through the loss of a loved one, a terrible medical diagnosis, or even week after week of a job you despise. Whatever has driven you towards these feelings, let the word of God restore your soul.

According to this verse, God's word gives life. Not a band-aid or a pep talk, but life: soul-rejuvenating, heart-restoring, hurt-healing life. When you're struggling in those moments, let the word of God do what it does best. God will comfort, encourage, and heal your heart through meditation on His word.

Dear God, life is hard sometimes. So hard, in fact, that I often don't know what to do or how to handle it all. Let these days drive me to Your life-giving word. Amen.

Psalm 119 - Delight in the Word

> *"for I find my delight in your commandments,*
> *which I love."*
> PSALM 119:47

I am overjoyed when I see my son succeed or my daughter continues to grow. I love spending time with my wife. Getting to sit down with a good book and a cup of coffee truly makes me happy. But here we are pressed to add another thing to the list of joys in our lives. The psalmist says that his delight is in the word of God. Then he doubles down by saying they are things that he loves.

What's on your list? What are a few of your favorite things? When you think about the Bible, do you have a favorite verse, character, or truth? I want to encourage you to develop your love of the word of God. Let it be numbered among the things you want to do and not just need or have to do.

Dear God, grow in me a love for Your word.
Let it be so sweet to my soul that I'm longing
for more time in it and with it. Amen.

Psalm 119 - Promises

"I entreat your favor with all my heart;
be gracious to me according to your promise."
PSALM 119:58

A pinky promise used to be the most unbreakable vow I could make as a kid. Who could ever forgive someone with the audacity to break a pinky promise? Unfortunately, we have all experienced broken promises. Beginning back in grade school until now, we find people who are unable or unwilling to keep their word. This betrayal of trust can be devastating to us and our relationships.

But God has never broken a promise. He has promised to save all who would place their faith in Jesus as their savior and lord. He has promised to never leave or forsake his people. He has promised to give wisdom to all who ask for it. The Bible is full of the promises of God, and not one has slipped his mind. We, like the psalmist, can confidently ask God to be gracious to us because it is according to His promise.

Dear God, I praise You that you have made and kept all Your promises to me. I trust that You will continue to be faithful and gracious. Amen.

Psalm 119 - Firmly Fixed

> *"Forever, O Lord, your word is firmly fixed in the heavens."*
> PSALM 119:89

Not only are the promises of God sure, but His plans are as well. Whatever the Lord decrees, it will come to pass. Like a solid foundation, it is firmly fixed and will not be moved. It does not bend and bow with changing conditions or cultures. What God has said is what He has meant.

This is a great encouragement for us as Christians today. We live in an ever-changing world. From technology to cultural values to views on spirituality, it seems as if nothing is absolute. But God's word stands firm where it was planted. We do not have to wonder where God stands on various issues, nor do we have to fret over how He feels about His people.

Dear God, Your word is unshakeable. Thank You for giving me such a firm foundation to build my life on. Amen.

Psalm 119 - Light unto My Path

"Your word is a lamp to my feet and a light to my path."
PSALM 119:105

We can see the progression of thought that is taking place throughout Psalm 119 as we near its end. He begins by explaining how he feels about God's Word. Then he gives different reasons why he delights in and is consumed by it. He explains that it is a trustworthy foundation and path worth following in light of these things.

When we face doubt, or question whether or not following what the Bible has to say is worth it, we can walk through Psalm 119 and come to the same conclusion the psalmist did. We can remind ourselves of the wondrous things that are within its pages. We can think back on its life-giving work in our lives. We can then trust that it will continue to light the way for us and keep us from stumbling.

Dear God, Your word is trustworthy and true. The path I walk in this life can be full of things that cause me to fall. Teach me to follow the light of Your word. Amen.

Psalm 119 - Consistent

> *"I hate the double-minded, but I love your law."*
> PSALM 119:113

The psalmist is making a strong and important point as we wrap up Psalm 119. He says that he hates the double-minded. That can be taken two different ways. It could mean those who have ulterior motives behind what they say and do. It could also refer to those who change their minds easily on vital issues. Either way, that type of person is hated by the psalmist.

Perhaps you can relate to those feelings if you've ever felt completely confused by someone's contradictory actions or statements. Double-mindedness is always hurtful and deceptive. The psalmist runs from that type of person to the most consistent, trustworthy one there is: God. He alone can say that His word is firmly fixed in the heavens. By His example and grace, let us strive to be strong in what we say and consistent in how we think.

Dear God, I confess that I am tempted to say what others want to hear instead of what they may need to hear. Help me to be truthful without being arrogant or belittling of others. Amen.

Meditate on the Word

"This Book of the Law shall not depart from your mouth, but you shall meditate on it day and night, so that you may be careful to do according to all that is written in it. For then you will make your way prosperous, and then you will have good success."
JOSHUA 1:8

Joshua was the successor of Moses. He led the Israelite nation through various battles to conquer the land of Cannan. That was the land that God had promised to give to His people generations beforehand. At the beginning of his leadership, Joshua committed himself to the word of God. In fact, he meditated on it. This means that he spent time thinking about it, chewing on it, mulling it over. He let it marinade his heart and inform his decisions. Like the first bit of a favorite dish, he savored it.

The promise accompanying this kind of dedication to God's word is prosperity. We need to be careful not to slip into a dangerous thought: if I read God's word every day, then all that I do will prosper. Generally, following Scriptural guidelines for life does bring a level of prosperity. If we do what God's word says, we can expect the outcomes that it promises.

Dear God, teach me to meditate on Your word. Help me to trust and follow it, knowing that the outcome is secured in You. Amen.

Breathed Out by God

> *"All Scripture is breathed out by God and profitable for teaching, for reproof, for correction, and for training in righteousness,"*
> 2 TIMOTHY 3:16

I want to highlight the very first word of this verse: All. What Paul is about to tell Timothy in this verse applies to all Scripture. This includes everything from the lists of laws to the apocalyptic passages to the narrated failures of Israel. According to Paul, every verse that we have in our possession is both from God and profitable.

In essence, God has given us a book from His very heart to transform ours. As we commit to studying the Bible, we can keep this truth tucked away. We can use it to ask ourselves, what is profitable for me about this passage? What do I need to learn? What in my life needs to change? God has promised that these verses are from Him and for us. Let's embrace that.

Dear God, I am so thankful that You would speak to me. You have given me Your word for Your glory and my good. Mold my heart with it. Amen

Compete and Equipped

> *"that the man of God may be complete,*
> *equipped for every good work."*
> 2 TIMOTHY 3:17

Following what Paul has already said about God's word being for our good, he gives us the goal of it all. It's for our completion and our equipment. When we find the word complete being used here, we have to remember that this verse was originally written in Greek, and sometimes the wording can get lost in translation. A better word for our understanding may be mature. The word of God works in us to mature us towards holiness, thus making us complete.

The second goal of Scripture is to equip us for good work. That means we cannot read the Good Book without being pushed to do good work. We cannot let our reading of Scripture become just another mental exercise. As James says, "Let us not be hearers only, but doers of the word."

Dear God, use Your word to mature and push me towards righteousness. Don't let my reading of it be just another thing that I do today. Amen.

Memorize the Word

> *"You shall therefore lay up these words of mine in your heart and in your soul, and you shall bind them as a sign on your hand, and they shall be as frontlets between your eyes."*
> DEUTERONOMY 11:18

As we have seen so far, the word of God is of vital importance for the believer. So the question then becomes, "How can we be sure to soak in God's word?" Moses encourages us to commit the word to memory through practical means. For the Jewish people at the time, these actions wouldn't have been culturally strange, but if we were to wear a headband with Bible verses on it, we might get a few strange looks.

I'm not suggesting that that is the best way to memorize Scripture. I am saying that there are practical, physical ways to regularly take in God's word. You can put a sticky note on your fridge that you have to recite each time you open it. You can put a note-card on your dashboard that you can practice reciting while you drive. Whatever creative idea you can come up with, go for it. Do whatever it takes to commit His life-changing word to memory.

Dear God, I struggle to hold Your word in my heart. Show me how best to commit it to memory. Amen.

Be Transformed

> "Do not be conformed to this world, but be transformed
> by the renewal of your mind, that by testing you may
> discern what is the will of God, what is good and
> acceptable and perfect."
> ROMANS 12:2

Have you ever felt jealous of Moses? He had the incredible, undeniable experience of speaking with God through a burning bush and on a mountain top. What about the disciples? They literally walked with Jesus and sat under His teaching. Have you ever wanted those experiences so that you could speak with God and get clarity on His will for your life?

The Bible teaches us that God speaks to us primarily through His word. It is what God uses to transform us by the renewal of our minds. It's what He will use to expose His will to our hearts. We have something that Moses and the disciples did not. We have God's full word in black and white before our eyes, and we have the Holy Spirit to guide us in it.

Dear God, I want to know Your will for me. I want to know You. By Your word, in the power of Your Spirit, reveal those things to me. Amen.

Eagerly Receive the Word

"Now these Jews were more noble than those in Thessalonica; they received the word with all eagerness, examining the Scriptures daily to see if these things were so."
ACTS 17:11

The book of Acts lays out for us the birth of the Church. Through it, we get to see how the gospel began to spread to all nations. As more and more people began to hear the good news of Jesus Christ, they had differing reactions. The response of God's people, however, was always the same. They "received the word with all eagerness."

This kind of language should sound familiar to us. It reminds us of the psalmist in Psalm 119. This eagerness or deep love for the word of God is a mark of genuine Christianity. This is not to say that if you have days of dryness, then you're not a believer. It is to say that if you've never hungered for the word, then you may not be a true disciple of Christ.

*Dear God, give me a hunger for Your word.
Let me receive it with eagerness, ready to
enjoy it every day. Amen.*

Two-Edged Sword

> *"For the word of God is living and active, sharper than any two-edged sword, piercing to the division of soul and of spirit, of joints and of marrow, and discerning the thoughts and intentions of the heart."*
> HEBREWS 4:12

There is no book like the Bible. There are incredible classics that can move our hearts and thrilling new books that can change our perspective. There are plenty of religions that hold tightly to a text that claims some kind of authority. But there is none like the word of God.

It stands alone. It alone is living and active. It alone is the book that reads us. It shows us our weaknesses and needs. It shows us the only cure for our troubles. It is the marvelous instrument of our God to work in His people. Let us not forsake the infinite value of the scalpel that God uses to do surgery on our lives.

Dear God, what a priceless gift You have given to me! Use Your word to cut to the core of my life and remove all that would displease You. Amen.

Freedom in the Word

*"and you will know the truth,
and the truth will set you free."*
JOHN 8:32

Growing up, I would play a board game where you could be sent to jail if you landed on the wrong spot. When I would be sent to jail, the wait to be set free felt like an eternity. I couldn't progress in the game until three turns had passed, or I rolled doubles with a pair of dice.

But the feeling of being set free so I could continue on was so great! This is how the word of God works for us. It's like a get-out-of-jail-free card. There's no more waiting and no more rolls of the dice. It shows us the key to freedom in Christ Jesus by giving us the gospel. As God uses His word in our lives, it breaks the chains of sin that have held us in bondage for so long.

Dear God, I praise You for the freedom You have given to me by Your word. Allow me to feel the full joy of that freedom today. Amen.

The Word Became Flesh

> *"And the Word became flesh and dwelt among us, and we have seen his glory, glory as of the only Son from the Father, full of grace and truth."*
> JOHN 1:14

God has always chosen to work through His word. In creation, He spoke and brought things into existence. He called Abraham to be the father of the nation of Israel by His word. He led His people through prophets and priests who presented His word. All along the way, we have rejected the word of God. So God took it a step further. His whole message of redemption and salvation that He had been speaking from the beginning, He sent in Jesus Christ.

The very word of God became flesh and lived among us. He did all the Father said He would. He lived a life and preached a gospel that was full of grace and truth. Still, mankind rejected the most personal word of God and had Him crucified. I urge you today, not to reject the word of God. It is full of grace and truth.

Dear God, forgive me for when I have rejected Your word. You have pursued a relationship with me, and I have turned away. Open my eyes to the grace and truth you have for me. Amen.

Abide in Him

> *"But the anointing that you received from him abides in you, and you have no need that anyone should teach you. But as his anointing teaches you about everything, and is true, and is no lie—just as it has taught you, abide in him."*
> 1 JOHN 2:27

Here we have an incredible promise! John, speaking of Jesus, says that when we place our faith in Him, and He abides in us, we don't need anyone to teach us spiritual things. How is this possible? If Jesus abides in us, then He is present to guide us towards truth as we study His word.

This doesn't mean that we will understand everything immediately. We all know experientially that that's not true. This also doesn't mean that there is no value in reading good books or listening to good sermons. We can benefit greatly from hearing what God has taught our brothers and sisters. This means that none of us cannot read, appreciate, and apply God's word for ourselves.

Dear God, thank You for being with me as I read Your word. I trust that You will help me to understand it as I need to. Amen.

The Key to the Bible

> *"You search the Scriptures because you think that in them you have eternal life; and it is they that bear witness about me,"*
> JOHN 5:39

Jesus gives us a key insight into understanding the Old Testament in this dealing with the Pharisees. He tells them that the whole Old Testament is ultimately about Him. When Isaiah wrote of the suffering servant in his fifty-third chapter, he was speaking of Jesus. When the promise that the serpent's head would be crushed was given in Genesis 3:15, God talked about Jesus. When the sacrificial system was laid out in Leviticus, it shadowed the ultimate Sacrifice to come in Jesus.

This revelation ought to color how we understand the Bible. It's not two separate books, but two volumes of one whole story. The Old Testament points us toward Jesus, and the New Testament points back to His ministry. The point of reading the Bible is not to know you but to know Jesus. And the more we can understand who Jesus is, the better we will understand this thing we call life.

Dear God, show us, Christ. Let us see him in every passage we read and every verse we memorize. Amen.

Set Your Heart

> *"For Ezra had set his heart to study the Law of the Lord, and to do it and to teach his statutes and rules in Israel."*
> EZRA 7:10

The ministry of Ezra was unique and difficult. He was part of the leadership of the people of God out of captivity and back to the Promised Land. Ezra's primary focus was on the temple's physical rebuilding and the spiritual rebuilding of God's people. He led them through the hard process of rebuilding the house of God and the painful process of repentance over sin.

This strong man's leadership started with one goal. He set his heart to study the Bible. He wanted to know and teach the will of God. This central thought guided everything that he did and all that he accomplished. This ought to be our guiding focus as well. Let all that we plan to do, and accomplish, be motivated by the word of God.

Dear God, this is the cry of my heart that it would be set to know You and Your word. Let Your word have its way in my life. Amen.

Blessed by the Word

"Blessed is the one who reads aloud the words of this prophecy, and blessed are those who hear, and who keep what is written in it, for the time is near."
REVELATION 1:3

John tells us in Revelation that we should be hearing God's word in two ways. We should be hearing ourselves speak it and hearing others speak it. If we do this, then we will be considered blessed by God. Not only are we to hear God's word in this two-fold way, but we are to keep it as well.

I would say that the best way to keep God's word is to be sure that we hear it in both ways. We need to regularly read God's word and even preach it to ourselves. We also need faithful brothers and sisters that are willing to speak God's word to us, even when it is hard to hear. Let's push towards these two goals so that we keep His word.

Dear God, provide me with a brother or sister who will faithfully bring Your word to my ears as I need to hear it. Help me to be that brother to someone else, I pray. Amen.

Spiritual Milk

"Like newborn infants, long for the pure spiritual milk, that by it you may grow up into salvation"
1 Peter 2:2

If you're a father, then you've heard the cry of an infant that can only be satisfied by its mother's milk. It is both a life-sustaining and nurturing process when a mother feeds her child. This is the way it is when we long for God's word. It both gives us life and fosters a relationship between God and us.

This relationship has its supernatural effect and causes us to grow up into salvation. In other words, we grow into our robe of righteousness. It's ours from our spiritual birth, but it doesn't seem to fit quite right until we mature and grow into it. I encourage you to continue to daily take in that life-giving, relationship-building word.

Dear God, what a unique experience I get to enjoy when I read Your word. It meets my needs and deepens my relationship with you. Thank You. Amen.

Grow in Grace

> *"But grow in the grace and knowledge of our Lord and Savior Jesus Christ."*
> 2 Peter 3:18

This is a summary of what discipleship is: to grow in the grace and knowledge of Jesus. For this devotion today, I want us to take a moment to examine our lives in two ways. The first is to ask the question of are we growing? Can we look back over the past couple of months or years and say that we have grown in some way? Are we less arrogant than we were before? Are we more sacrificial for our families? Are we more devoted to our wives?

The second way is to consider how we are making disciples of other men. We ought to be asking ourselves if we have helped anyone else grow in this grace and knowledge. If not, then what is keeping us from this task? Maybe we need to ask ourselves who God has placed in our lives for this purpose?

Dear God, I thank You for having grown me since my salvation. I pray that you will use me to disciple and grow other brothers in the faith. Amen.

A Sure Bet

> *"so shall my word be that goes out from my mouth; it shall not return to me empty, but it shall accomplish that which I purpose, and shall succeed in the thing for which I sent it."*
> ISAIAH 55:11

Every bet I've ever taken, I've lost. I'm not sure why my "luck" seems to be so bad when it comes to games of chance. Even when I thought I had a sure bet, things always seemed to fall through for me. In reality, there are very few things we can count on.

God makes clear through his prophet Isaiah that His word is a sure bet. Whatever He declares will come to pass. We see this clearly in creation where He said, "Let there be," and there was. God uses His word, which has made promises to us and has determined what our future will hold. We're in good hands.

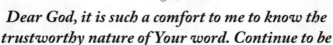

Dear God, it is such a comfort to me to know the trustworthy nature of Your word. Continue to be faithful to me. Amen.

Encouraged by the Word

> *"For whatever was written in former days was written for our instruction, that through endurance and through the encouragement of the Scriptures we might have hope."*
> **ROMANS 15:4**

Is the Old Testament still relevant? This is a question that many people will wrestle with as they work their way through the Old Testament and find many of the cultural practices outdated and the Law fulfilled by Christ. Why do we still need the Old Testament?

Paul gives us two reasons in this verse. The first is for our instruction. We can learn many things from the examples of different people. From Genesis to Malachi, we can observe what to do and what not to do. More importantly, we can see the foreshadowing for Christ on every page. We ultimately see how Jesus is the better Adam, Abraham, Moses, or David. The second reason is that we might have hope. Our hope comes from our knowledge of who Jesus is in light of the Old Testament. We must resist the temptation to overlook the first half of the BIble because it is hard to understand or relate to. It's there for our instruction and hope.

Dear God, teach me through Your word. Fan into the flame the hope I have in Jesus through the Old Testament. Amen.

⇒ Day 90 ⇐

Danger of Forgetting

> *"My people are destroyed for lack of knowledge;*
> *because you have rejected knowledge, I reject you from being*
> *a priest to me. And since you have forgotten the law of your God,*
> *I also will forget your children."*
>
> **HOSEA 4:6**

The people who should know God and His word the best were God's people. On top of that, the ones who should rise above the rest should have been the priests. They regularly were supposed to teach others about God's word. But here the indictment of God against His people. He pronounces punishment because they have rejected knowing Him.

Brother, let this be a sobering warning to us. We have access to the most important document to ever be written. Whenever we desire, we can crack it open and hear from the Almighty God of Creation. May we never stray away and forget Him, His goodness, and the sacrifice of His Son.

Dear God, remind me daily of Your grace to me.
Speak to me through Your Word that I
may never forget you. Amen.

Dwell with the Word

"Let the word of Christ dwell in you richly . . ."
COLOSSIANS 3:16

For the past thirty sessions, we have discussed all the implications of what it means to be a strong man in the Lord who studies God's word. Let's take a moment to wrap up that concept. What can be our prayer for ourselves and for our fellow brothers who are fighting to be strong in the Lord?

Let's take Paul's phrase in Colossians 3 and pray it back to the Father. Let's desire that the very words of Jesus would dwell in us. The world that dwells there is used to paint a picture of someone moving into the neighborhood. Let's allow the word of Christ to take up residence in our hearts and dwell there richly. His word will have its effect on our lives and will conform us to His image.

Dear God, I pray that the word of Your Son will dwell richly in my brothers and sisters and in me. Amen.

Strong Men
Declare

Teach the Word

> *". . . teaching and admonishing one another in all wisdom, singing psalms and hymns and spiritual songs, with thankfulness in your hearts to God."*
> COLOSSIANS 3:16

Paul follows up the admonition to let the word of Christ dwell richly in you with the natural response to that: a declaration. If you soak up the word, at some point, it'll be time to let it all out. Whether that's through teaching, singing, or thankful prayer to God, the word of God will not be able to be contained within you.

Communicating God's word takes boldness and strength. Sometimes what God's word has to say about a situation will not be taken well. In fact, at times, it can be downright offensive to someone else. Like Jesus, we will need to balance our truth with grace, but we cannot omit the truth. Over the next few weeks, let's take a long look at what it means to be strong in the Lord and declare His word to others.

Dear God, provide me the grace and strength to spread Your word, the truth for all. Amen.

Rightly Divide the Word

> *"Do your best to present yourself to God as one approved, a worker who has no need to be ashamed, rightly handling the word of truth."*
> 2 TIMOTHY 2:15

The mark of someone who is approved of God and a worker on His behalf is someone who rightly handles the word of God. In other words, he declares today what God has declared in the past. He doesn't change the message or bring his own, but He rightly handles God's word on His behalf.

This admonition was originally given to a pastor named Timothy, but pastors are not the only people who can handle the word. When people come to us for advice or they are looking for guidance in a certain area of life, we are commissioned by God to respond with His word and not our own. Let's be approved workers and rightly divide the word.

Dear God, I need Your help if I'm going to handle Your word well. Give me wisdom. Amen.

Give a Defense

"but in your hearts honor Christ the Lord as holy, always being prepared to make a defense to anyone who asks you for a reason for the hope that is in you; yet do it with gentleness and respect,"
1 PETER 3:15

One of the many scenarios you might have to handle the word is when someone asks you why you believe. I have been put in that position many times in my life. Some of those times, I have been left speechless. It was a horrible feeling to have someone press my faith and not give a defense.

Although this cannot always be avoided (because we cannot have all the answers to all the questions), we can fight against it by being as prepared as possible. If nothing else, we can always defend the hope that is in us by the testimony we have of God's grace in our lives. We don't have to have all the answers, or all of our theological stances figured out. We just need to be confident that Jesus has changed our lives and tell about how and why.

Dear God, don't let me be defenseless. You have saved me and changed me. Bring those thoughts to my mind if I need to stand my ground when someone tests my faith. Amen.

Ready to Explain

> *"So Philip ran to him and heard him reading Isaiah the prophet and asked, "Do you understand what you are reading?""*
>
> ACTS 8:30

When we will need to handle the word, someone has a genuine question about the Bible. This is not an opportunity to give a defense but to go on the offensive and persuade someone to follow Jesus.

In this scenario, Phillip saw someone reading the book of Isaiah with a confused look on his face. He ran into the situation, ready to help the man understand what He was reading. Ultimately, that man came to know Jesus and was saved and baptized that day. Largely because a man was ready and willing to rightly divide the word for someone who needed help. We can be that instrument in God's hands too.

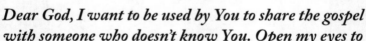

Dear God, I want to be used by You to share the gospel with someone who doesn't know You. Open my eyes to the opportunities and help me to be prepared. Amen.

Teach Your Children

> *"You shall teach them diligently to your children. . . "*
> DEUTERONOMY 6:7

The first mission field we have to declare God's word is in our homes. It can be easy for us to set our sights on our friends or co-workers when considering who we ought to share God's word with. Although we ought to do that, we cannot forget those closest to us who will receive it even better than those other people in our lives.

Many of us get the privilege of teaching our kids the good news of Jesus Christ. If that's you, I want to encourage you to take that opportunity with pride. You can make disciples right under your own roof. Be intentional and flexible as you teach the Bible to your kids. Some days and even some ages are easier to teach than others. Lean on your spouse for help and work towards that common goal.

Dear God, You have given me a mission field in my living room. Help me to take the initiative and teach my children about You and Your word. Amen.

Daily Life

> "... and shall talk of them when you sit in your house, and when you walk by the way, and when you lie down, and when you rise."
> DEUTERONOMY 6:7

When we think about declaring God's word to our children, we can tend to think about a formal Bible study or family devotion time. Those times are good and important to have, but notice how Moses presents teaching to our children. He says to do it throughout the day. He wants the word of God to be a regular part of life, not an event at the end of the day.

So the next time you're at the park, and you see the trees, talk to your kids about the creator of the trees. If you see a firetruck or ambulance racing down the road, take that opportunity to pray with your kids for the people involved. According to Moses, thinking about and discussing God's word needs to be as normal as walking and talking.

Dear God, forgive me for not making Your word a priority in my house. It's not as natural of a thing to talk about as it ought to be. Guide me in leading that effort in my home. Amen.

⇒ Day 98 ⇐
Practical Steps

> *"You shall bind them as a sign on your hand, and they shall be as frontlets between your eyes."*
> DEUTERONOMY 6:8

When it comes to teaching God's word to others, often more is caught than taught. This means that your kids will get more out of seeing your trust, study, and live out God's word than just hearing you talk about it. You setting the example for them is as important as you preparing the family devotion.

When Moses speaks about binding them on your hands and on your head, he refers to a method of memorizing and beholding God's word in a public way. Take efforts to let your kids see you read and be changed by the Bible. Talk about what God is teaching you at the dinner table. Be a worthy example for them to follow.

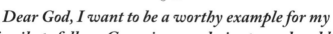

Dear God, I want to be a worthy example for my family to follow. Grow in me a desire to read and be changed by Your word. Amen.

Day 99

Holistic Teaching

> *"You shall write them on the doorposts of your house and on your gates."*
> DEUTERONOMY 6:9

I have tried to lose weight a handful of times, and I'm usually willing to make a change to do that. Sometimes, I'll eat better. Sometimes I'll go to the gym regularly. But each time, what is necessary for success is a holistic approach. I need to change my way of life to see long-lasting results.

The same is true for teaching our children God's word. This is what Moses is trying to get across to us. We cannot just talk about it with our kids. And cannot be content to just be an example for them. We need to let God's word and a desire to teach it to permeate our entire lives. This desire will reach all the way out to how we decorate our house! Everything we do and every decision we make will be influenced by this desire.

Dear God, I want to declare Your word well to my family. I want to be intentional in doing so. Give me wisdom as I pursue this goal by Your grace. Amen.

Train Up a Child

> *"Train up a child in the way he should go;
> even when he is old he will not depart from it."*
> PROVERBS 22:6

As we wrap up thinking about teaching the Bible to our kids, we see the benefit of it from Solomon in his proverbs. He says that how kids are raised is how they will stay. In other words, if we teach them to love God, love others, and share the gospel, then that's what they will do when they get older.

For many of us, this is our hope for our kids. Of course, we wish them happiness and success, but more than that, we pray they will be faithful followers of Jesus Christ. Because this is a proverb and not a promise, we need to taper our expectations of how all of this will play out. But generally speaking, these things are true for us. Brothers, this is worthy work we do. Press on.

*Dear God, help me to labor well in the hard work
of raising children in the Lord. Keep them in
Your grace as they grow and begin to make
independent decisions. Amen.*

The Great Commission

> *"Go therefore and make disciples of all nations, baptizing them in the name of the Father and of the Son and of the Holy Spirit, teaching them to observe all that I have commanded you. And behold, I am with you always, to the end of the age."*
> MATTHEW 28:19-20

This is the Great Commission. The final command that Jesus gave His disciples and the very purpose of the Church today. All believers are called to take part in this endeavor. We are not to be spectators in the stands or players on the bench. We are to be on the court, gameplan in mind, and courage in our hearts.

While we cannot forget our home, as we have discussed already, we cannot stop at our home either. There is a world of lost men and women who are in desperate need of the gospel. Our job is to boldly go and declare this good news to those who don't believe in their salvation and those who do believe in their encouragement. Let's follow our King into battle and declare His word.

Dear God, I have a daunting task before me. It feels impossible to accomplish. Teach me to rely on Your grace and presence as I share Your word with those around me. Amen.

Declare with Integrity

> *"Show yourself in all respects to be a model of good works, and in your teaching show integrity, dignity, and sound speech that cannot be condemned, so that an opponent may be put to shame, having nothing evil to say about us."*
> TITUS 2:7-8

One of the top complaints that nonbelievers have about Christianity is hypocrisy. They are told or at least get the impression that Christians are perfect people who live perfect lives and spend all their time judging others for their shortcomings. This misconception of the Christian faith is partly due because men have taught them without integrity.

They have declared that God loves them, and yet they are unwilling to love them. They proclaim that judging others is wrong while wagging their fingers. Brothers, let our lives and words be ones of integrity. Let us speak God's word in such a way that we cannot be put to shame or have anything evil said about us.

Dear God, let my speech and actions be a right reflection of Your word. I will fall short. When I do, teach me to confess and repent before those I have hurt. Amen.

Just Like You

> *"A disciple is not above his teacher, but everyone when he is fully trained will be like his teacher."*
> LUKE 6:40

"I want to grow up to be just like you." These are some of the sweetest and most challenging words my son has said to me. It's an honor that someone would want to be like me, but I know me. I know my sinful heart and the ways I have hurt people in the past. There are times when it scares me to think that there will be another me out there one day.

As we share God's word with our friends and family, we are calling them to follow us as we follow Christ. This means that they will grow in our strengths but will also be slow in our deficits. As disciples, we need to be aware of our limitations and our need to grow in a community of believers who round us out.

Dear God, it is an honor to have someone look up to me spiritually. Help me to use that opportunity wisely and be willing to look to others for help. Amen.

Gentle Words

> *"May my teaching drop as the rain, my speech distill as the dew, like gentle rain upon the tender grass, and like showers upon the herb."*
> DEUTERONOMY 32:2

Moses had a goal for how his teaching would come across. He wanted to be like rain or dew in the morning. He wanted it to be gentle, abundant, and life-giving. This doesn't mean that Moses never rebuked or had hard conversations with God's people. After coming down from the mountain, he smashed the tablets containing the Ten Commandments in anger at the sinfulness he saw. But when he began to speak, his goal was humility.

Sometimes, we can have a temptation to be more like a thunderstorm than a rain shower in our sharing of God's word. We might come crashing down in judgment or scare others by intimidation. The next time we have the opportunity to provide correction, let's ask ourselves, "How will my tone and posture be received when I say these words?"

Dear God, I confess that I can thunder and rage easier than I can be gentle and soft. May my words be like gentle rain upon the tender grass. Amen.

Disciple-Making Disciples

> *"and what you have heard from me in the presence of many witnesses entrust to faithful men, who will be able to teach others also."*
> 2 TIMOTHY 2:2

Paul was instructing Timothy, a young pastor when he wrote this letter. His primary intent was for Timothy to raise up fellow elders or pastors to serve. However, the principle here applies to all disciples of Jesus. We are to make disciples who make disciples.

This means that we have more than immediate results in mind. We are looking to the future generations to come and thinking about how they will be impacted by what we do today. We are trying to grow God's kingdom in a sustainable way that won't abruptly end with our inevitable passing away. Let's think bigger than ourselves and past our lives for the glory of God.

Dear God, give me a vision for generations to come. Help me to bear them in mind as I make my choices today. Amen.

Sound Doctrine

"But as for you, teach what accords with sound doctrine."
TITUS 2:1

As we declare God's word and make disciples in different ways, we have this charge from Paul. He encourages us to teach only the accords with a sound doctrine. Like a train that must run on its tracks to avoid calamity, we must be steadfast in staying in line with what is right.

If two people set out in the same direction, but one decided to go one degree more to the right, eventually, they would end up miles apart. The deceptive thing about that is, for miles, they will be so close that they won't notice the drift before it's too late. Let's constantly readjust and set our sites back on sound doctrine so we will not drift and carry others away in our wake.

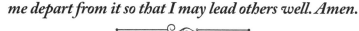

Dear God, give me a burden for sound doctrine. Do not let me depart from it so that I may lead others well. Amen.

Truth in Love

> *"Rather, speaking the truth in love, we are to grow up in every way into him who is the head, into Christ,"*
> EPHESIANS 4:15

If you've ever watched a singing competition on television, then you have seen different judges speak the truth. Some speak it without gentleness and bring the competitor to tears. Some speak it with so much sugar-coating that competitors won't learn from their mistakes.

Paul says that we are to speak the truth in love. This means that what we say and how we say it is governed by our love for the other person. This means that you don't sugarcoat the truth, but you also do not wreck the other person in the process. We must speak with a gentle tone, a genuine heart, and a steady hold to the truth.

Dear God, help me to speak the truth in love.
I admit that I do not do this well at times.
Forgive me and grow me. Amen.

Practice What You Preach

*"you then who teach others, do you not teach yourself?
While you preach against stealing, do you steal?"*
ROMANS 2:21

Practice what you preach. This may be the most important lesson for us to learn as strong men who declare God's word. It will all be for naught if we don't do what we say for others to do. Our credibility and even our salvation might be called into question if we say one thing and do another.

How can we trust someone's advice on marriage if theirs is falling apart? Why should we believe someone that Jesus will forgive all our sins if they don't forgive their neighbors? What you say and what you do bear incredible weight. Brothers, as the old saying goes, let's practice what we preach.

Dear God, I confess that I don't live my life perfectly. I desire to practice what I preach. Help me to do that. Amen.

Know Your Student

> *"For though by this time you ought to be teachers, you need someone to teach you again the basic principles of the oracles of God. You need milk, not solid food,"*
> HEBREWS 5:12

How would you teach a child to change a tire? What about an adult? You would do it in completely different ways. You would use simple language and provide a lot of assistance and grace for a child. You would push the adult to do as much as possible independently to learn it for themselves.

When it comes to making disciples, the people we encounter will be on different levels of maturity. Some will be able to handle the solid food that Paul refers to. Some will be brand new Christians that need the basic milk of the word. Others, sadly, will be older, immature Christians who have never been discipled. They, too, will need basic principles taught to them. Take time to assess where you are on that spectrum.

Dear God, I pray that You would help me to grow in maturity. Give me the wisdom to understand where I am, and other people are in their walks with You. Amen.

⇒Day 110⇐
Carnivore Christianity

> *"But solid food is for the mature, for those who have their powers of discernment trained by constant practice to distinguish good from evil."*
> HEBREWS 5:14

How do we make the transition from milk to solid food? What do we need to do and teach others to do to grow in this way? The author of Hebrews gives us some insight. He says that it takes constant practice. This means that it requires work. It also means that it takes time.

We may desire and feel like we are ready for solid food, but that won't be true until we have put in the work and time it takes. This means that when we begin to disciple someone and declare God's word to them, we are making a commitment to them. We tell them that we are willing to do the work with them, and we are ready to give them our time and energy. Let's honor that commitment and hold them accountable as well.

Dear God, declaring Your word is work. It takes time and energy that I don't always have. Give me the strength to raise solid-food-eating brothers and sisters. Amen.

Always Be Ready

"preach the word; be ready in season and out of season; reprove, rebuke, and exhort, with complete patience and teaching."

2 TIMOTHY 4:2

When I was in high school, I used to wrestle. I remember one match where my opponent and I were evenly matched. We were almost out of time, and it was going to come down to a matter of points. All I had to do was stay away from him for a few seconds and avoid being taken down. My coach called out to me, "Get your hands up! Be ready!" Immediately after the whistle was blown, my opponent shot in to tackle me to the ground, and all of a sudden, my world was in slow motion. I thought to myself as I fell to the mat; I can't believe I wasn't ready for that.

Paul's exhortation to Timothy here is to always be ready. We don't know when our next opportunity to declare God's word will come. Let's make an intentional effort to be on our toes and be prepared for whatever may come our way. Let's listen to our coach and be ready.

Dear God, I get tired and distracted. Keep me alert and ready to serve You at all times. Amen.

Taught by God

> *"for the Holy Spirit will teach you in that
> very hour what you ought to say."*
> LUKE 12:12

Maybe you have been hesitant to try to make disciples because you don't know what you'll say when it happens. Maybe you're concerned that you won't have the right words to say when someone begins to share their burdens with you or ask your advice.

Let me offer you this incredible piece of encouragement. The Holy Spirit was promised to be with you and teach you what you ought to say. It may not always go perfectly or happen in the way that you'd like it, but you will not be left to fend for yourself. When those moments come when you don't know what to say, say just that. Tell them that you don't know, but God does, and you will do all you can to help them figure it out.

*Dear God, I need Your help if I'm going to help others.
I need Your words to offer counsel and wisdom,
not my own. Amen.*

You are the Man

> *"Nathan said to David, "You are the man! Thus says the Lord, the God of Israel, 'I anointed you king over Israel, and I delivered you out of the hand of Saul.'"*
> 2 SAMUEL 12:7

In this dramatic scene, Nathan is boldly confronting king David regarding his sin. David had an affair and had the husband killed to cover it up. Nathan goes to him and tells him a story about a wealthy man who habitually stole from a poor man. Nathan asked what he thought should happen to the wealthy man. David said that he should surely die. Then Nathan delivered the harsh truth to David when he said, "You are the man!"

There will be times in our lives where we will have to be strong and bold to confront our friends in their sins. This would have been particularly daunting for Nathan to do because he could have been put to death for speaking this way to a king. But he loved his friend more than his own life and spoke the truth. Do you have that kind of love for your neighbor?

Dear God, give me the boldness and love to speak like Nathan did to David. Help me to understand I'm only one decision away from his position. Amen.

Passing the Torch

> *"Then Moses summoned Joshua and said to him in the sight of all Israel, "Be strong and courageous, for you shall go with this people into the land that the Lord has sworn to their fathers to give them, and you shall put them in possession of it."*
> DEUTERONOMY 31:7

Passing the torch to your predecessor is a precious and powerful moment. Before the whole nation of Israel, of whom Moses was the leader, he commissions Joshua to finish the work he started and lead them into the Promised Land. We can imagine the weight and significance of the moment for Joshua and how he hung on every word from Moses.

There will probably only be a handful of moments like this in our lives. That is when we will need to declare God's word carefully and wisely. Moses told Joshua the thing he needed to be reminded of those most; that his strength and courage to go forward come from the promises of God. When given these opportunities, let's push our brothers and sisters towards the trustworthy word of God.

Dear God, You use me daily in different ways. There are coming days where You will use me to significantly impact someone's life. Prepare me for those days. Amen.

⇒Day 115⇐

A Father's Instruction

"Hear, my son, your father's instruction, and forsake not your mother's teaching, for they are a graceful garland for your head and pendants for your neck."
PROVERBS 1:8-9

Whether biologically or relationally, many of us will have the opportunity to be a father figure in someone's life. Solomon had sons and wrote the book of Proverbs for their benefit. He wanted to pass along the wisdom that God had given him over his lifetime.

What a privilege for some of us to play that role in someone else's life. I want to encourage you to not take that lightly. God has placed someone in our paths to pour into so that we can see them grow into who God would have them to be. We get to be instrumental in someone trusting Jesus deeply and loving God fervently. This kind of investment will have a return in our lives, as well as we rejoice in the good work that God has done.

Dear God, use me as a vessel of Your wisdom and grace. I'm honored to be used by You. Amen.

The Message We Declare

"this Jesus, delivered up according to the definite plan and foreknowledge of God, you crucified and killed by the hands of lawless men."
ACTS 2:23

As we close out our time thinking of how strong men declare the word of God, I wanted to define our message. What is it that we ought to be boldly declaring to our friends and families? What message both saves the lost and makes disciples of those who believe? It's none other than the Gospel of Jesus Christ.

Peter begins his message by leaning on the never-changing word of God. He says that the work of Jesus was a definite plan of the Father. This message we proclaim and believe is sure and trustworthy from the very beginning. We have no reason to doubt or shrink back when declaring this good news.

Dear God, thank You for always being faithful to keep Your word. Help me to be bold as I declare it to others. Amen.

⇒Day 117⇐

The Power of God

> *"God raised him up, losing the pangs of death, because it was not possible for him to be held by it."*
> ACTS 2:24

Not only do we have confidence in the trustworthiness of the message we declare, but we also have tremendous hope. Who else can say this? Who else is loved by a God with this magnitude of power? The God we follow has conquered death! This is such a sweet encouragement that we can offer to our brothers and sisters who feel like they cannot overcome the circumstances in their lives.

This is the message that we get the honor of proclaiming to a spiritually dead world. There is hope for them! By God's grace, He can raise their souls from the dead if they will only trust in the resurrection of His Son.

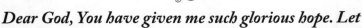

Dear God, You have given me such glorious hope. Let that hope radiate in my words and my deeds. Amen.

Both Lord and Christ

"Let all the house of Israel therefore know for certain that God has made him both Lord and Christ, this Jesus whom you crucified."
ACTS 2:36

Now Peter presses this glorious, hope-filled message into the people's lives in a way that they cannot ignore. He is putting something before them that they cannot turn a blind eye to. They must respond in some way. He is saying to them that Jesus is both the long-awaited Christ and the Lord of all. And so now they must either reject Him as Lord, even in light of the evidence before them or accept Him.

This is the kind of pressure we ought to have with declaring the gospel. It is a good thing to lay out the evidence in a winsome and convincing way. It is a good thing to help people appreciate the grace shown to them in Jesus' death and resurrection. But we cannot stop there. We must declare Him as Lord over all and press our hearers to do something with that truth. By God's grace, that will accept and follow Him.

Dear God, don't let our conversations die too soon. Give us the opportunity to call those in our lives to respond to Your gospel. Amen.

Repent and Be Baptized

> *"Now when they heard this they were cut to the heart, and said to Peter and the rest of the apostles, "Brothers, what shall we do?" And Peter said to them, "Repent and be baptized every one of you in the name of Jesus Christ for the forgiveness of your sins, and you will receive the gift of the Holy Spirit. "*
> ACTS 2:37-38

Upon the conviction of the Holy Spirit through the preaching of the gospel, the people responded and said, "What now? We believe. What do we do now?" Peter then tells them to turn from their sins and be baptized. This follow-up encounter is vitally important to the health of a new believer. They need someone to answer them when they ask, "What now?"

We can be that person. We can be there to continue to show them the depths of the gospel and how it not only saves them but sanctifies them. It doesn't just break the chains of sin and death. It pulls us to our feet and sets us on the path of righteousness. It fuels our bodies as we pursue holiness. In other words, it allows us to be strong in the Lord and in the strength of His might.

Dear God, put us in the gap. Let us be there when someone comes to faith and needs to know the next step. Help us to strongly declare Your word. Amen.

Strong Men

Love

Love Your Wife

> *"Behold, you are beautiful, my love; behold, you are beautiful; your eyes are doves."*
> SONG OF SOLOMON 1:15

Choosing to love someone every day takes strength. There are days when they won't seem lovely, and you won't feel like being loving. These days we have to rely on the strength that God provides to love them well. We are going to begin our study by thinking about how to love our spouse well.

There may not be a better book to study for this topic than the Song of Solomon. It is a love song between a man and a woman who love each other dearly. As we work our way through it, we will take notes from what the man has to say about his wife.

Dear God, teach me to love my wife well every day. I need Your grace. Amen.

A Special Love

*"As a lily among brambles,
so is my love among the young women."*
SONG OF SOLOMON 2:2

Solomon expresses his love for this woman by more than just calling her beautiful, as we read before. Although that is important, there are deeper things to note about our significant other. Here Solomon notes that she stands out among the crowd. She's like a beautiful flower in a thorn bush. In comparison to all around her, she is stunning.

When we can see and notice what makes our spouse stand out, that shows them that we think they are special. This gives love to them because that means they are in a different category altogether in your mind. There's everyone else on the one hand and then your precious lily on the other.

Dear God, I want my wife to know how special she is to me. Help me to communicate my feelings to her today. Amen.

Worth Finding

> *"King Solomon made himself a carriage from the wood of Lebanon. He made its posts of silver, its back of gold, its seat of purple; its interior was inlaid with love by the daughters of Jerusalem."*
> SONG OF SOLOMON 3:9-10

In the third chapter, Solomon is gone. He has taken his army off to war. On this day, he and his men are supposed to return. The woman searches all over for the one she loves. Then all of a sudden, Solomon and his men appear on the hilltop. It says that he made the various things that he brings with him.

The thing to note about this passage is that Solomon was making himself worthy of being found while the woman was looking for him. He made himself and what he had to offer the very best he could provide. We need to strive to be worthy of being found by our wives. Each day we come home, let's bring the best version of ourselves to her to show our love.

Dear God, I want to be found as someone worthy. I can only do this by Your mercy and grace. Be kind to me, I pray. Amen.

Come with Me

> *"Come with me from Lebanon, my bride;*
> *come with me from Lebanon."*
> SONG OF SOLOMON 4:8

One way that people feel loved is by spending time with them. Whether your destination is to view the mighty cedars that Lebanon was known for or to simply go to the store, inviting your spouse to come along with you communicates a lot.

It says to her that you want to spend time with her. It shows that you find her presence enjoyable or comforting. By inviting her to be with you, you're inviting her into your life. You're saying to her, "I want you."

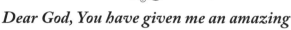

Dear God, You have given me an amazing
wife to love. Teach me to show her how
much I want her in my life. Amen.

⇒Day 124⇐

Captivated My Heart

"You have captivated my heart, my sister, my bride; you have captivated my heart with one glance of your eyes, with one jewel of your necklace."
SONG OF SOLOMON 4:9

Do you remember the day that your wife captivated your heart? Think back to that moment. What was she doing that made you think, "I love her." It's a love that stole his attention and kept it. Here Solomon is expressing that kind of love to his bride.

It can be difficult to find the right words to say, but it is so meaningful when we put in the effort to do so. Our actions are not always enough to communicate our deep feelings for our wives. We need to commit to doing the work or sorting through and expressing our love to our wives.

Dear God, I love my wife, and I don't always do a great job telling her that in meaningful ways. Help me to express those thoughts to her. Amen.

Beloved Friend

> *"This is my beloved and this is my friend,*
> *O daughters of Jerusalem."*
> SONG OF SOLOMON 5:16

The relationship between husband and wife should be summarized by two words: beloved and friend. We have discussed how we need to express to our wives that they are beloved by us. But the marriage relationship isn't all romantic, intimate moments.

It includes laying around and watching television together, enjoying hobbies together, laughing together. When we get married, it should be to our beloved friend. The person who is the most important to us and whose company we enjoy the best.

Dear God, in my wife, You have given me a beloved friend. Thank You for that precious gift. Amen.

Proud Love

> *"You are beautiful as Tirzah, my love, lovely as Jerusalem, awesome as an army with banners."*
> SONG OF SOLOMON 6:4

As the king of Israel, when Solomon says that she is as lovely as Jerusalem (the capital city) and as awesome as an army with banners (under his command), it is more meaningful than we realize at first glance. Because we are not kings or leaders of armies, we need to put ourselves in Solomon's shoes to better understand. When a king looks out over his kingdom or his army, he is filled with pride. He sees the love of his people and the obedience of his soldiers.

When Solomon says this about his loved one, he is filled with pride over her. He sees her strength like an army. He sees her beauty like a great city. We, too, ought to behold our wives with such pride. Not only should we appreciate it for ourselves, but we should communicate that to her as Solomon did.

Dear God, I am proud of the wife You've given me. By Your grace, You've brought us together. Help me to appreciate that daily. Amen.

Sacrificial Love

> *"Husbands, love your wives, as Christ loved the church and gave himself up for her,"*
> EPHESIANS 5:25

As with every topic in Scripture, it all comes back to the gospel. Paul encourages us to love our wives with sacrificial love. Jesus was willing to endure an excruciating death on the cross out of His love for His people, for us. This is the example of love we have to follow.

We can think about it in a theoretical way and ask ourselves, "Would I take a bullet for my wife?" That would produce some good thoughts and evaluations. But a better use of our time today might be to ask, "Would I fix dinner for my wife?" You see, Jesus wasn't just willing to die for His Church. He lived to serve it as well. If we're willing to take a bullet but not take out the trash, what kind of love is that?

Dear God, foster my love for my wife.
Give me a sacrificial heart for her so I can
serve her however she needs. Amen.

With Your Heart

> *"You shall love the Lord your God with all your heart. . ."*
> DEUTERONOMY 6:5

Our love for our wives comes from the foundation of our love for God. Any love that we have to offer must be grounded in our love from and for the Father. Let's take a few days to think about what it looks like to love the Lord your God with all your heart, all your soul, and all your might.

To love with all your heart means to put your whole emotional being into it. It doesn't just mean that you should only feel love for God. It means that when you honor, trust, fear, and respect God, you're loving Him as well. Let us, with all the emotions that God has given us, love Him wholeheartedly.

*Dear God, all of my hopes, fears, trust,
and love I give to You. You alone are worthy
of this kind of allegiance. Amen.*

Day 129

With Your Soul

". . .and with all your soul. . ."
DEUTERONOMY 6:5

Who are you? Have you ever been asked that question? It can cause us to stop for a minute and think about who we are at our core. When we drill down to the center of our being, what we will find is our soul. Mysteriously, God has hardwired our minds and our souls to create the very nature of who we are.

So, to love the Lord our God with all our soul is to give back to Him what Has created. It's to say to Him, "Lord, You have formed and fashioned me with such love and care, I commit it all to Your use. All my skills and shortcomings, I offer to You to use how You see fit." Have you made that kind of commitment to God? Have you loved Him in that way?

Dear God, all that I am, I give to You.
Use me for Your glory and my good. Amen.

With your Might

> ". . . and with all your might."
> DEUTERONOMY 6:5

If loving God with your heart is your thought and feelings while loving Him with your soul is the core of your being, then loving Him with your might is with all that you do. These things are inseparable. What the command in Deuteronomy is calling for is holistic love from us.

This means that everything we do should be an act of love towards God. When we read our Bibles, we're loving God. When we work heartily as unto the Lord, we're adoring God. When we care for our families, we're showing our care for God. And so, brothers, I charge you: love the Lord your God with all your heart, with all your soul, and with all your might.

Dear God, this is my desire: to love you fully.
You have loved me fully through Your Son,
and so I give my life in return. Amen.

Obedient Love

"If you love me, you will keep my commandments."
JOHN 14:15

Obedience is not love. We can obey out of fear. We can obey out of selfish intent. We can even obey to manipulate the one being obeyed. Obedience is not always characterized by love. However, we cannot love God without obedience.

Obedience is a sign of our love for the one we are obeying. It secures our motivation and protects us from twisting its purpose for it. When we seek to obey God's word, particularly the difficult commands, let's plant our feet more firmly in love. This is the ground we stand on and the very reason for our obedience in the first place.

Dear God, I love You. Because I love You, I want to obey You. Show me what You would have me to do. Amen.

One Love

> *"No one can serve two masters, for either he will hate the one and love the other, or he will be devoted to the one and despise the other. You cannot serve God and money."*
> MATTHEW 6:24

If you were to ask a college basketball fan who they pulled for, you would never find someone who said, "I pull for Duke University and UNC-Chapel Hill!" In the sports world, those two teams are mortal enemies. You cannot pull for both teams and still have integrity as a sports fan.

We find a similar truth when it comes to following Jesus. Ultimately, we can only have one love, one master. We can surely love our wives, families, even jobs, and hobbies, but our ultimate love can only be one thing at the end of the day. If you were forced to choose between Jesus and your wife, where would your allegiance fall? If you had to pick between confessing Christ and keeping your job, would you still be employed? Challenge yourself today with these thoughts.

Dear God, there is room for only one King on Your throne. Forgive me for the times that I have tried to replace You with lesser things. Amen.

Love Like Jesus

> *"A new commandment I give to you, that you love one another: just as I have loved you, you also are to love one another."*
> JOHN 13:34

Do you remember the WWJD bracelets? They were colorful bracelets with those letters on them that stood for "What Would Jesus Do?" There was a time where this slogan was plastered on every Christian item known to man. The American Christian would have been taken by the thought of what Jesus would do in any given situation.

Regardless of the situation, it is Jesus' very nature to love. He would choose to love others in the circumstance would vary, but the motivation in His actions would be a love for the Father and a love for His people. We need to ask ourselves if this is how we operate? Do we love as Jesus loves? Do we allow that love to penetrate everything that we do?

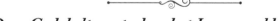

Dear God, help me to do what Jesus would do. Help me to have love at the center of all of my actions. Amen.

Brotherly Love

> *"And this commandment we have from him:*
> *whoever loves God must also love his brother."*
> 1 JOHN 4:21

Brothers can be hard to love. I have a twin brother and an older brother. We have had our share of disagreements and arguments along the way. It's hard enough to love family, let alone the "brothers" that John refers to in this passage. Here, John is talking about anyone who is a believer in Jesus, both male and female.

When we place our faith in Jesus, we are adopted into his family. Because Jesus' gospel has extended to so many cultures, ethnicities, and socio-economic levels, the church is full of very different people. Those differences can make it difficult to love one another. When those difficulties present themselves, we must remember what has brought us together, our united love for God because of His gospel.

Dear God, let me never lose sight of the gospel.
It is the thing that unites my brothers and me together.
Help me to love them out of that. Amen.

Selfless Love

> *"Do nothing from selfish ambition or conceit, but in humility count others more significant than yourselves."*
> PHILIPPIANS 2:3

Don't breathe! Impossible, right? Breathing is so natural that we don't even think about it. If we were to try to hold our breath, we'd eventually pass out and begin to breathe anyways. It's just what we do. When Paul tells us to do nothing from selfish ambition, it's like he is saying, "Don't breathe!"

We are sinfully and naturally selfish. We are driven to do what's best for us and keep ourselves at the top of our priorities. Everything that we do, even kind things for others, is often laced with selfish motives. This is why we must be strong in the Lord and His strength to do this. We need a new heart and supernatural guidance to consider others more significant than ourselves. We must rely on the grace of God to live this way.

Dear God, You have shown me selfless love in sending Your Son to die for me. Teach me to use that as fuel to love others selflessly, too. Amen.

Forgiving Love

> *"Above all, keep loving one another earnestly,*
> *since love covers a multitude of sins."*
> 1 PETER 4:8

As believers, we've all been faced with the challenge of forgiving someone. Sometimes it's easy because the offense was unintentional or not that big of a deal. Other times, the offense was malicious and calculated. When those times come, it can feel impossible to forgive, and we surely won't forget it. How do we forgive when the stakes are this high?

It all comes back to our love for one another. We are to have a love for all people. This love isn't the same for all people, but it's there for all people. We look at our neighbors with the eyes of Christ; compassionate and kind. When we view the party that has wronged us as Jesus has, we see their desperate need for forgiveness from the Father as more important than our issue with them. That greater love sweeps over the offense and brings about forgiveness.

Dear God, give me the strength to forgive those who have wronged me. Remind me of the great forgiveness that I have been shown by You. Amen.

Honoring Love

> *"Love one another with brotherly affection.*
> *Outdo one another in showing honor."*
> ROMANS 12:10

I love competition. It doesn't matter if it's a game of tennis or dominoes. I put all that I have into the game. So, when Paul says to outdo one another, I'm ready to lace up! But the Christian life is not a competition with winners and losers. It's also not a life of being a spectator. It's a lifestyle dedicated to doing the most good to the most people for the glory of the Most High God.

So when Paul says to outdo one another, take up the challenge. Don't compare your efforts to another for the sake of judging. Put your efforts next to another to hold your own feet to the fire. Be challenged and encouraged by other brothers and sisters that are doing good work for the glory of God.

Dear God, grow a desire in me to outdo my brothers and sisters in showing honor. Not for my glory, but for Yours, I desire to do this. Amen.

Witnessing Love

> *"By this all people will know that you are my disciples, if you have love for one another."*
> JOHN 13:35

There are countless methods of evangelism. There are acrostics that you can use to share your faith. There are tracts you can walk people through. There are conversation guides you can utilize. And all of those options can be helpful and good. However, Jesus says that one of the best witnesses of your discipleship of Jesus is simply loving one another.

Why would that be such a mark of Christianity? Because we live in a world where it is uncommon to love others who are different from you. When you receive Jesus as Lord, you're also receiving His diverse Church. He calls us to love one another. When the world sees your love for all people, they will wonder what's different with you. Then you can share the gospel in this unique way.

Dear God, for Your glory and for the sake of the watching world, help me to love others well and without preference. Amen.

Friendly Love

*"A friend loves at all times,
and a brother is born for adversity.."*
PROVERBS 17:17

I have brothers and friends that are like brothers. One of the big differences between the two is that our friends choose to be in our lives. Our family doesn't necessarily do that. So when the proverb says that a friend loves at all times, that's exactly right. If they are our friends, they are choosing to love us. They are choosing to be in our lives.

So what I want to challenge us with today is to be that friend. Be the friend that is choosing to love. Be the friend that is choosing to forgive when they are hurt. Be the friend that is choosing to sit with someone through a hard time. Be the friend that rejoices with the success of others, even if you're not succeeded. Let's be that kind of friend.

*Dear God, teach me to be a good friend. Give me
the strength to do the hard work of choosing to love
someone regardless of the circumstances. Amen.*

⇒ Day 140 ⇐
All-Encompassing Love

> *"Let all that you do be done in love."*
> 1 CORINTHIANS 16:14

If love has the effects that we have been talking about: it offers forgiveness, shares the gospel, follows in Jesus' footsteps, then it's clear that all we do needs to be directed by love. Paul, speaking to the broken Corinthian church, gave them this command. He was exhorting them to leave behind their divisions and arrogance to pursue a love for one another.

Just as Jesus taught us about the Law, its summary is love. Love God and love our neighbors as ourselves. So let's strive to love. Let our motivations, thoughts, and actions be guided along by love as a kite is guided by the wind. Let love carry us along.

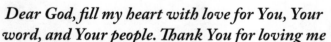

Dear God, fill my heart with love for You, Your word, and Your people. Thank You for loving me unconditionally. Amen.

Working Love

> *"Jacob loved Rachel. And he said, "I will serve you seven years for your younger daughter Rachel."*
> GENESIS 29:18

Now that we have a full understanding of what love is and what love does let's see it in action. Over the next few days, we will see how people in the Bible expressed their love in significant ways. We are benign with the love that Jacob had for Rachel.

In this incredible story, Jacob strikes a deal to marry Laban's daughter, Rachel. He agrees to a 7-year contract of service for her hand in marriage. After the seven years are over, Laban tricks Jacob and gives him his older daughter, Leah. Jacob, refusing to accept this but unwilling to dishonor his uncle Laban, agrees to work another seven years for the opportunity to spend his life with Rachel. Jacob's love for her drove him to incredible lengths to secure a future with her. Challenge yourself in light of this kind of love.

Dear God, teach me to have and express this kind of love for my significant other. Let my love for them overcome any odds. Amen.

Special Love

> *"Now Israel loved Joseph more than any other*
> *of his sons, because he was the son of his old age.*
> *And he made him a robe of many colors."*
> GENESIS 37:3

Jacob, now called Israel, loved the people in his life deeply and distinctly. In his own family, his son Joseph was the apple of his eye. Whether right or wrong, he loved Joseph with a special kind of love among his brothers.

I'm not going to argue that you ought to love one of your children more than another. I believe there was a fault in how Israel treated his sons. However, I do want us to notice that his love for Jacob was unique and special. So should our love be for those in our lives? Because every relationship is different, find out what is special in it. Rejoice in the unique love you can have for different people in your life.

Dear God, You have given me so many different people to love. I love them for different reasons and in different ways. Let me rejoice in these differences. Amen.

Redeeming Love

"Then the women said to Naomi, "Blessed be the Lord, who has not left you this day without a redeemer, and may his name be renowned in Israel!"
RUTH 4:14

The love story between Ruth and Boaz cannot be done justice in this short devotional. I encourage you to take a few minutes and read it in its entirety. Being only four chapters long, it is an investment well worth your time. The core of the story is the concept of redemption.

The widowed Ruth was redeemed by Boaz due to his love for her. He saw her service to Naomi, her work ethic, and that she had been so moved by the word of God that she left her home country to love among His people. He saw what was lovely about her specifically and pursued her. Let's never stop pursuing our spouses. Let's look for what makes them lovely and love them all the more for it.

Dear God, You have given me someone who is incredible to love. Help me to pursue her every day. Amen.

Godly Love

> *"For God so loved the world, that he gave his only Son, that whoever believes in him should not perish but have eternal life."*
>
> JOHN 3:16

Let's take a moment and marvel and the display of God's love for us. The perfect, holy, infinite God of all creation who owes nothing to us gave Himself the most precious person, His Son. He gave this wretched world Jesus to have and abuse and mistreat for His life. He gave us Jesus to wrongly accuse and crucify. He gave us Jesus to execute His gracious plan of redeeming His people by the life, death, and resurrection of His Son. May we never forget, He gave us Jesus.

And in light of this great gift, we must believe in Him and receive the free gift of eternal life. There is no other right response to such an irresistible offer. True life, abundant life, and life with Christ are ours for the taking if we simply believe. So, I urge you, believe! Place your faith in a God who loves his people sacrificially and will do all things for our good and His glory.

Dear God, I believe! Help my unbelief. Grow in me a better understanding and appreciation for the deep love You have for me. Amen.

Yearning Love

> *" For God is my witness, how I yearn for you all with the affection of Christ Jesus."*
> PHILIPPIANS 1:8

Paul has a deep, yearning love for the Philippian church. He was involved in the church's foundation and, as an apostle, has helped them grow and function rightly. Even as Paul has continued his journey or church planting and sharing the gospel, he has kept in touch with this sweet group of people.

Perhaps you can relate to this situation. Maybe you are or have been a part of a local church that has gained your affections. Sunday morning gatherings are a joyous occasion for you as you get to regather with your brothers and sisters in Christ. If you don't have that experience, I encourage you to seek out a local church to be known by and to know. This is a special bond reserved for God's people. Don't miss out on it.

Dear God, thank You for placing me in my local church. Show me how to enjoy that community and love it in return. Amen.

⇒Day 146⇐

Deep Love

> *"As soon as he had finished speaking to Saul, the soul of Jonathan was knit to the soul of David, and Jonathan loved him as his own soul."*
> 1 Samuel 18:1

There may not be a deeper friendship found in Scripture than that between David and Jonathan. This unlikely pair went through difficult trials as Jonathan's dad, king Saul, wanted to have David killed. Jonathan went as far as to deceive his father to protect David's life. As it says in God's word, their souls were knit together.

What a blessing from God it is to have a friend like this in our lives. Someone who understands us and knows us, and doesn't reject us when times get tough. I'm going to challenge you to take time today to thank God for that friend that He has placed in your life. On top of that. I want you to send that friend a text or give them a phone call and let them know how much you appreciate them and why.

Dear God, You give me good gifts. I'm so thankful for this friend that you have put into my life. Amen.

Child's Love

> *"Then Shem and Japheth took a garment, laid it on both their shoulders and walked backward and covered the nakedness of their father. Their faces were turned backward, and they did not see their father's nakedness."*
> **GENESIS 9:23**

Everybody makes mistakes. In this story, we find Noah, fresh off the ark that God used to save him and his family, passed-out-drunk on the floor. This is not the Bible story that he is most known for, but it was part of his life. What is significant about this passage is the love and honor shown to Noah by two of his sons. Lying in his filth and nakedness, the sons walked backward into the room to cover their father.

People that are close to us that we love and respect are going to fall short. They will make a mistake that will challenge what you think about them and maybe even cause you to lose some respect for them. Let's be like Shem and Japeth. Let's preserve the dignity of the one who has fallen and assume the best as often as we can.

Dear God, teach me to give grace to those who make mistakes. I know a greater grace has been given to me by You. Amen.

Motherly Love

> *"When she could hide him no longer, she took for him a basket made of bulrushes and daubed it with bitumen and pitch. She put the child in it and placed it among the reeds by the river bank."*
> EXODUS 2:3

Sometimes, the strongest example of love is not found in a man but in a mother. In this beautiful story, Moses' mother places all her faith in God and all her love towards her son in a basket. There was a mandate from the Pharoah to have all of the firstborn male children to be thrown into the Nile river for their execution. Ironically, Moses' mom uses that river for her son's protection.

The combination of faith in God and love for another makes the strongest presentation of love. It's these two things that drove Jesus to the cross. Because of these things, God raised Him from the dead. And in light of these things, we love our neighbors as ourselves.

Dear God, instill in me this kind of love that is borne from faith in You. Let me show it to others today. Amen.

Strong Men

Sing

The First Love Song

> *"This at last is bone of my bones and flesh of my flesh; she shall be called Woman, because she was taken out of Man."*
> GENESIS 2:23

Christians are singing people. All throughout Scripture, we find faithful men and women singing bold songs of God's strength. In the book of Psalms, we have a book of songs that His people have sung and continue to sing today. Therefore, it would be wise for us to look at these songs and the strong men who have sung them.

The first is the song of Adam. He has been looking for a suitable life partner. He goes through all the animals, and none are sufficient. So God puts him to sleep and creates for him a woman named Eve. When he opens his eyes and sees her, he bursts into a song of awe and thankfulness. From the very beginning, men have been singing praises to God. Let's not stop now.

Dear God, You give us plenty of reasons to sing. Help to see those and give You praise for them. Amen.

Sing of Triumph

"I will sing to the Lord, for he has triumphed gloriously;
the horse and his rider he has thrown into the sea."
Exodus 15:1

This was an incredible moment for the people of God. After leaving their captivity in Egypt, they were chased by Pharaoh's army. God miraculously split the Red Sea, leaving a dry path for His people to cross over to safety. Pharaoh's army tried to pursue only to have the walls of the sea come crashing down on them, wiping them out. It was an incredible display of power, and Moses led His people to sing in response to it.

We have countless examples of the display of God's power in His word and in our lives. Each one of these events is tuning our hearts to sing of His great triumph. Let's respond to His works in this good and right way. Let's praise and glorify our God.

Dear God, inspire me towards worship again. Open my eyes so that I will see Your great works. Amen.

⇒ Day 151 ⇐

Sing of Strength

> *"The Lord is my strength and my song, and he has become my salvation; this is my God, and I will praise him, my father's God, and I will exalt him."*
> EXODUS 15:2

Once again, we see the theme of this book presented clearly in the word of God. The people sing, "The Lord is my strength." And who would dare argue this point with them? God has single-handedly defeated the enemy of His people. What felt to them like a tidal wave of power was to Him, flicking a drop of water from His finger.

Our strength, the strength that we rely on to live this Christian life, comes from this powerful God. When we feel exhausted, overwhelmed, or powerless, we can take comfort in this source of strength. We will not exhaust this great resource. We cannot overextend the might of our God.

Dear God, You are mighty beyond our comprehension. There is no good thing that you cannot do. Teach me to rely on that strength. Amen.

Sing of Holiness

"Who is like you, O Lord, among the gods?
Who is like you, majestic in holiness,
awesome in glorious deeds, doing wonders?"
EXODUS 15:11

These are rhetorical questions because the answer is obvious. There is no one like our God. No one can do the great and awesome things that He can do. No one loves His people as fiercely as He does. He is holy, distinct, set apart from all creation because He is the Creator.

His holiness alone grants us reason to worship Him. But He has not stopped with revealing that about Himself. He has pursued us and loved us. He has shown a desire to protect and preserve His people for His own purposes. Let's rest in that truth today. That same God, who parted the sea for Israel, works to preserve and protect us today.

Dear God, You are for me. What an amazing
truth to behold. Allow me to appreciate that
more and more. Amen.

Sing of Leadership

> *"You have led in your steadfast love the people whom you have redeemed; you have guided them by your strength to your holy abode."*
> EXODUS 15:13

Have you ever wandered through a corn maze? It can be frustrating and fulfilling simultaneously as you try to navigate the confusing landscape. If you're at a large corn maze, there is often a map available or a man in a tower to offer assistance for you. I can remember going through one and waving my flag for help. The man in the tower, being able to view the whole course, gave clear direction on how to get to the end.

Our God has a clear view of the whole corn. In fact, He made the maze and set us in it. We get the privilege and honor of having direct communication with the only One who can lead us rightly through this life. Let's lean on His guidance through prayer, His Word, and godly counsel from trusted brothers or sisters in Christ.

Dear God, I am waving my flag. I don't know where to go and what to do. Make clear the path You would have me take. Amen.

Sing of Security

"You will bring them in and plant them on your own mountain, the place, O Lord, which you have made for your abode, the sanctuary, O Lord, which your hands have established."
EXODUS 15:17

C an you remember the feeling of being held by a parent after a nightmare? At that moment, there is nothing and no one else who could make you feel safe, like your mom or dad. There is a familiarity to them and an inherent trust.

This is how it is with our God. He is leading us toward safety. He offers to be our refuge. While the people of Israel were headed to a physical place of solace, we are offered an imminent spiritual reality. We are offered refuge for our weary souls in Christ. Take God at His word today and find rest in Him, your Lord.

Dear God, my rock and my redeemer.
You offer me safety and security in You.
Let me run to You in my time of need. Amen.

⇒Day 155⇐

Sing of His Reign

> *"The Lord will reign forever and ever."*
> EXODUS 15:18

Egypt was not the only kingdom that the Israelites had to deal with. Throughout their history, they would have issues with Philistia, Assyria, Babylon, and more. There was a constant threat to the throne of their kings. They would ebb and flow in their ability to fight off the enemy as well as their obedience to God.

In their shifting and swaying, God remains constant. No matter who is in office or who sits on the throne here, God alone occupies the throne of Heaven. And He will reign for all of eternity. We can have hope in our future through bleak times, knowing that none of it is outside of His control. We have a good and gracious King.

Dear God, my allegiance and my life I submit to You.
Nations will rage, and kings will rise and fall,
but You will remain. Amen.

Song of David

> *"Saul has struck down his thousands,*
> *and David his ten thousands."*
> 1 SAMUEL 18:7

King David wrote many songs recorded in the book of Psalms. But there was one song that was written about David. This was before he became king, and Saul was on the throne. As David was returning from battle, the people would sing this refrain. This deeply disturbed Saul because he was fearful he would lose the throne to David. However, when they sang his praises, David didn't puff out his chest and lifted his head high. He constantly gave glory to God for his successes.

Sometimes, the action that takes a great deal of strength from us is to give glory where it's due. Ultimately, everything that we accomplish in life is due to God's grace. When people began to sing our praises, let's redirect the focus to the One whom the honor is truly due: our God.

Dear God, thank You for how You've given me success in life. Teach me to point others to You. Amen.

Song of Lament

> *"And the king lamented for Abner, saying, "Should Abner die as a fool dies? Your hands were not bound; your feet were not fettered; as one falls before the wicked you have fallen."*
> 2 Samuel 3:34

Songs of lament can be found in various parts of the Scriptures. These come up when a person is heartbroken over a situation and expresses their sorrow in the song. Although not many of us lament through song, we can identify with the emotions that produce these songs. David lamented over the untimely death of his son.

I pray that none of you have experienced this kind of heartache as you read this devotional today. However, I know that there are some of you who have gone through something like this in this broken world. I encourage you to lament. Be open and honest with God and lean on Him for strength. I'm deeply and truly sorry that you have gone through such an awful experience.

Dear God, I'm angry and sad and confused.
Give me the freedom to express how I feel to
You and comfort me. Amen.

⇒Day 158⇐

Song of Remembrance

> *"I am distressed for you, my brother Jonathan; very pleasant have you been to me; your love to me was extraordinary, surpassing the love of women."*
> 2 SAMUEL 1:26

Not too many devotions back, we spoke about the deep friendship that existed between David and Jonathan. Unfortunately, Jonathan died at a relatively early age as well. And as was David's custom, he responded to these deep emotions with song. In this song, he takes time to remember Jonathan.

This is a good practice for us today. Not that we necessarily need to compose a song in honor of a loved one who has passed away, but we should actively seek to remember them. There are great men and women who have gone before us and are worthy of remembering. Some of them were close to us, and some we may have never known personally, but we have been affected by their lives. Take time to remember those men and women today.

Dear God, You have used so many men and women to shape and influence my life. Thank You for those people. Help me to not forget who they were and the lessons I've learned from them. Amen.

⇒ Day 159 ⇐

Song of Praise

> *"For this I will praise you, O Lord, among the nations, and sing to your name."*
> PSALM 18:49

When you think of singing in relation to Christianity, these are the thoughts that come to mind. It's a group of men and women who have chosen to praise God and sing to His name. This type of refrain can be found over and over in the Psalms. This is the heartbeat of the Christian life. We can find reason after reason to sing praises to our God.

I want to press you to do just that: sing! When you're at church in the midst of worship, sing along. When you're in the car on the way to work, sing songs that glorify God. When you're working around the house, sing in your heart to God with your headphones on. Brothers, we do ourselves, and those around us tremendous good when we choose to sing aloud our hearts desire for God.

Dear God, I will praise you and sing to Your name. Great are You, Lord, and greatly to be praised. Amen.

Song of Jehoshaphat

> *"And when he had taken counsel with the people, he appointed those who were to sing to the Lord and praise him in holy attire, as they went before the army, and say, "Give thanks to the Lord, for his steadfast love endures forever."*
>
> 2 CHRONICLES 20:21

Imagine this. You're surrounded by enemies who are stronger and larger than you. You're the king of your nation, and it's on you to defend your people. What do you do? King Jehosaphat called out to God in prayer. And God, in His kindness, answered him and said, "The battle is nor yours, but God's." And as surely as God had said it when the time came to fight, the battle was won for Israel. Not by their strength or might, but by God's.

In response to this kind of protection by God was to send out a victory band. He sent them before the army to sing of the love of God. This was a great reminder for the men who had fought to know where their victory came from. Let's remind ourselves daily that our victories are from the Lord. While we may fight, He gives the strength. And so, by His grace, let's sing.

Dear God, help me not to lose sight of You and how You're working in my life. Send a victory band before me to remind me of Your love. Amen.

Song of Isaiah

> *"Let me sing for my beloved my love song concerning his vineyard: My beloved had a vineyard on a very fertile hill."*
> ISAIAH 5:1

Through the prophet Isaiah, God sings a song for His beloved: us. He compares how He cares for us to how a gardener would care for a vineyard. What we need to highlight from this verse is that God sings over us. His love for us is so great that it brings him to joyful singing.

As we dwell on this thought, it should drive us to awe and wonder. How could a God so holy love sinful people like us? Why would God spend His time thinking of us? We may never fully understand the answers to these questions, but they are wrapped up in the person and work of Jesus Christ. He can love us because Jesus has bought us with His own blood. He spends time thinking of us because we are now His treasured people.

Dear God, who am I that you would be mindful of me? What grace you have shown me today. Amen.

Song of Peace

*"You keep him in perfect peace whose mind is
stayed on you, because he trusts in you."*
ISAIAH 26:3

What is the perfect peaceful moment for you? If you're a parent, you may not have experienced one of these in a long time. But if you could picture peace, what would be there? Is peace a walk along the beach? Is it indulging in a sweet treat while watching your favorite television show? Is it settling down with a good book? In this song of Isaiah, he sings of a promise of peace.

Peace comes from a mind that is stayed on God. That means that no matter what life throws at us, we are focused on our heavenly Fathers. As the author of Hebrews puts it, we are to fix our eyes on Jesus. Take steps towards this goal through prayer, reading the Word, or even singing songs of peace.

*Dear God, I want my mind to stay on You because You
are trustworthy. Help me to block out the distractions
of the world around me. Amen.*

Song of Judgement

> *"But the vine was plucked up in fury, cast down to the ground; the east wind dried up its fruit; they were stripped off and withered. As for its strong stem, fire consumed it."*
> EZEKIEL 19:12

This song of judgment is not going to be on the Billboard Top 100 anytime soon. It does not uplift or encourages. Ezekiel will not be going on tour with this album. So what's the point for us today? What do we have to learn from this?

It reminds us of a right fear of God. Yes, He loves us dearly. Yes, He sent his own Son to forge the path of the right relationship with us. But we must keep into perspective the might, holiness, perfection, and just wrath of God. This fear should be mixed with reverence, awe, and respect. Although Abraham was considered a friend of God, he still felt the weight of being in His presence. Let us not forget that either.

Dear God, forgive me if I have entered into Your presence too lightly. You are the great God of all creation. I want to honor You in how I speak to You. Amen.

Song of Life

> *"For thus says the Lord to the house of Israel:*
> *"Seek me and live;"*
> AMOS 5:4

This is the cry of our God, "Seek me and live!" It's like we are stranded in a desert, and our only chance of survival will be an oasis. And yet, we sit and make cups of sand, hoping that our circumstances may change. God is calling out from the oasis for us to come and drink.

Friend, if this is you, seek Him and live! If you are exhausted from life and have no joy or hope, you can find that in Jesus. He is the revival that your soul needs. He is the satisfying drink that you've been longing for. Do not wait another moment; run to His word and seek Him there. You will find Him with arms wide open.

Dear God, I'm done! I'm done begrudgingly going through this life. I want You and all that You offer Your people. Give me life! Amen.

Song of Joy

> *"Though the fig tree should not blossom, nor fruit be on the vines, the produce of the olive fail and the fields yield no food, the flock be cut off from the fold and there be no herd in the stalls, yet I will rejoice in the Lord; I will take joy in the God of my salvation."*
>
> HABAKKUK 3:17-18

In his book, Habakkuk has an honest conversation with God about what's going on in his life. He cannot understand how God would allow His people to come under attack by enemy nations. He brings complaint after complaint to a holy God. God then pulls back the curtain and reminds Habakkuk that He alone sees the full picture. He reminds Him of His promise to never let His people be fully destroyed. After this promise is firmly planted in Habakkuk's heart, he sings this song.

Here we find the great joy of the Christian life. While life circumstances are not what we would want, we can find joy in the ultimate promise of love for God's people. He will not leave us or forsake us. He will not let us be crushed. So let's rejoice together with Habakkuk in the God of our salvation.

Dear God, remind me of Your promises. Give me the right perspective on life and lead me to rejoice. Amen.

Song of the Ages

> *"And they sang a new song, saying, "Worthy are you to take the scroll and to open its seals, for you were slain, and by your blood you ransomed people for God from every tribe and language and people and nation, and you have made them a kingdom and priests to our God, and they shall reign on the earth."*
>
> REVELATION 5:9-10

In John's book, Revelation, we get a picture of what the end of time as we know it will look like. There are terrifying sights and confusing truths for us to wrestle with as we work through those passages. But one thing I want us to see is that part of the final plan of God includes His people still singing His praises for all of eternity. This is because He is eternally worthy of that praise.

Like the worship in this passage, our praise will be centered around the gospel. We will sing of the great sacrifice of our Lord, Jesus. We will rejoice in the reach of His work to pull in people from every tribe, language, tongue, and nation. We will worship our King for the rest of our existence. What a future we have in Him.

Dear God, today, I give You the praise and honor due Your name. Today and forever, I seek to give You glory. Amen.

Song of Hezekiah

> *"Then Hezekiah commanded that the burnt offering be offered on the altar. And when the burnt offering began, the song to the Lord began also, and the trumpets, accompanied by the instruments of David king of Israel."*
> 2 CHRONICLES 29:27

God's people had a rollercoaster relationship with Him. They were constantly up and down. They would be obedient for a season under a righteous king and then rebellious under an ungodly king. The seasons of righteousness seemed to dwindle as time went on, and there stood in their place longer seasons of ungodliness. This was not the case for king Hezekiah. During his reign, he sought to reinstate right worship in the temple.

What temple worship looked like was practically very different from how the Church worships. They would offer sacrifices and sing songs as the sacrifices burnt. Today, we sing about a sacrifice that was given once for all. We sing in light of a sacrifice made for us, not one we have to offer today. Let's rejoice in that wonderful truth today.

Dear God, thank You for the sacrifice of Your Son for me. I want to praise You for that gift today. Amen.

Song of Jesus

> *"And when they had sung a hymn,*
> *they went out to the Mount of Olives."*
> MATTHEW 26:30

Not long before His crucifixion, Jesus had supper with His disciples. Before this meal, He washed His disciples' feet. There He predicted His betrayal by Judas, who was sitting at the table with them. He led them in what we call the Lord's Supper or Communion. He told how His body would be broken, and His blood would be shed for the New Covenant God was making with His people.

It was an incredible evening, to say the least, but it did not end there. After eating the meal together, they all joined together in song. This is simply the way of God's people. When we commune with God, our response is to praise Him. Let's follow Jesus in this way. Let's be people that sing.

Dear God, You have been so kind to me. You have made a new covenant with me by the blood of Your Son. Help me to sing Your praises today. Amen.

⇒Day 169⇐

Power of Singing

> *"About midnight Paul and Silas were praying and singing hymns to God, and the prisoners were listening to them,"*
> ACTS 16:25

Paul and Silas sat in jail for preaching the gospel. In rusted chains and dirt floors, likely sitting in their own filth, they had a different disposition from everyone else. While the other prisoners were trying to mentally escape their circumstances or had hardened their hearts towards hope, Paul and Silas sang. They sang of the goodness of God.

What happened next is nothing short of a miracle. The ground shook with such force that the jail cell doors flew open. And then they perpetuated their peculiarity. They did not run towards freedom. They sat and waited for the jail guard to come by. Why? So they could then share the gospel with him. Brothers, let this be a lesson to us. The gospel changes everything from our attitudes to our actions.

Dear God, instill in me the faith and joy that was in Paul and Silas. When I'm in my harshest conditions, would You give me a song to sing? Amen.

Songs of Paul

*"Great indeed, we confess, is the mystery of godliness:
He was manifested in the flesh, vindicated by the Spirit,
seen by angels, proclaimed among the nations,
believed on in the world, taken up in glory."*
1 TIMOTHY 3:16

Paul was a man who was so moved to sing that even when he was writing different letters to the churches, he was involved with, he would include a short song of praise. Over the next few devotions, we will take a look at those songs.

In the first doxology, he rejoices in the mysteries of the gospel. Mysteries like how God could take on flesh, how this simple message would change the world, and how Jesus would be resurrected and taken up in glory. There are so many things to ponder as believers. Instead of those things giving us doubt, let's take the approach of Paul. Let them inspire wonder and awe in our God.

*Dear God, some things in the Bible are a mystery to me.
I know they aren't a mystery to You. Teach me to
rejoice in that. Amen.*

Gospel Singing

> *"And being found in human form, he humbled himself by becoming obedient to the point of death, even death on a cross."*
> PHILIPPIANS 2:8

It should come as no surprise to find that Paul's central theme is the gospel of Jesus Christ. Here he exalts Jesus for his humility. It truly is a marvelous thing to consider; that God Himself would leave the perfection of glory to pursue a relationship with rebellious and ungrateful mankind.

His humility did not stop at leaving heaven but submitted Himself to the excruciating and humiliating death on a cross. Above all of that, He endured the wrath of God for all who would believe in His work on the cross. Is there anything else we can do other than sing for joy?

Dear God, the sacrificial death of Your Son inspires my worship! Teach me to join with Paul in being amazed by His humility. Amen.

Song of Creation

> *"For by him all things were created, in heaven and on earth, visible and invisible, whether thrones or dominions or rulers or authorities—all things were created through him and for him."*
> COLOSSIANS 1:16

Once again, our brother is thinking of Christ as he bursts into praise. This time, however, he is meditating on the idea that Jesus is our creator. What I want to point out this time is the last two words in that verse, "for Him."

We were created for Jesus. To serve and glorify Him. At His good pleasure is the very purpose of our existence. Some of us may do this as carpenters, businessmen, entrepreneurs, or even pastors. God calls us to specific jobs and tasks in life, but at the end of the day, our ultimate purpose is to be His.

Dear God, bless me with the fortune of serving for Your purpose. Whatever I do is in the Name of You. Amen.

195

Song of Glory

> *"He is the radiance of the glory of God and the exact imprint of his nature, and he upholds the universe by the word of his power. After making purification for sins, he sat down at the right hand of the Majesty on high."*
> HEBREWS 1:3

The author of Hebrews composes one of the most beautiful verses regarding who Jesus is. He calls his first the radiance of the glory of God. If you can remember, back to Old Testament teachings, men could not see the full, unbridled glory of God and still live. The greatest visual representation of the glory of God, then, is Jesus.

He also calls Jesus the exact imprint of the nature of God. He is quite literally the eternal God in finite flesh. This mind-boggling truth is only made more glorious when the author recounts his actions. He made purification for sins (no light task) and then sat down (as if to say the work is done) at the right hand of the Father. Mull, over the words of this verse and let them fill your soul today.

Dear God, what a glorious insight into Your Son You share with me in Your word! Help me to appreciate it more and more. Amen.

Song of the Shepherd

"For you were straying like sheep, but have now returned to the Shepherd and Overseer of your souls."
I PETER 2:25

"Prone to wander, Lord, I feel it. Prone to leave the God I love! Here's my heart, Lord, take and seal it. Seal it for Thy courts above." These are the lyrics to a beautiful old hymn entitled Come Thou Fount. They capture beautifully this relationship found in our verse today. We are like sheep. We are prone to wander and do what we think is best. But God is our Shepherd and Overseer (or Pastor).

This is what our souls so desperately need. We need a good shepherd who is looking over us and caring for us. We need someone who will search for us when we stray away. Praise God. We have those things in Jesus, our Savior.

Dear God, I admit I am prone to wander, and so I ask that you would keep shepherding my soul. Amen.

Song of the Thanksgiving

> *"The Lord is my strength and my shield; in him my heart trusts, and I am helped; my heart exults, and with my song I give thanks to him."*
> PSALM 28:7

As we end our section on strong men who sing, there's no better place to look than the book of Psalms. This is a literal book of songs that were sung by the Israelites and the early church. Great, godly men have sung these songs for ages, and it only seems right that we join in.

In this Psalm, the purpose of it is to give thanks to God. I don't know what season of life you're in or what you're dealing with right now, but I want to encourage you to seek opportunities today to give thanks to God. There are likely some of you who are dealing with horrible life circumstances and cannot fathom giving thanks today. Can I encourage you to read the psalms and seek the heartache of the authors? Many are filled with tears and then rounded out with hope.

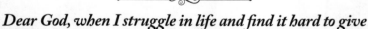

Dear God, when I struggle in life and find it hard to give thanks, show me Your word. Comfort me in it. Amen.

A New Song

> *"He put a new song in my mouth, a song of praise to our God. Many will see and fear, and put their trust in the Lord."*
> PSALM 40:3

I love music. I play guitar and lead in worship at my local church, so music is an everyday part of my life. One of the great joys of being a music lover is stumbling across a new song that you love. When that happens, you listen to it repeatedly and let the music and the lyrics take hold of you for a few days.

When the psalmist says that God put a new song in his mouth, I can imagine that it was that kind of experience. Not that he was listening to an online music streaming platform, but that God put a new reason to worship Him in his heart. And he put that reason on repeat and allowed it to take hold of him for a few days. May God give you a new song today.

Dear God, give me a new song to sing to You. Show me another reason to give You praise today. Amen.

⇒Day 177⇐

Song of Exultation

> *"I will be glad and exult in you; I will sing praise to your name, O Most High."*
> PSALM 9:2

To exult means to feel or show triumphant elation or jubilation. It's the feeling we get when our favorite football team wins in the last second. It's the moment our child takes their first steps. It's the experience of when our significant other says, "Yes!" when we are down on one knee. We get to exult in the triumph of our God.

Through the life, death, and resurrection of Jesus, sin and death have been defeated. Satan and his rule have been thwarted. The eternal God has fixed a time in history for all of His foes to be placed under His feet. As His children, we are co-heirs with Christ. We get the great joy of exulting in Him and sharing in His triumph.

―❦―

Dear God, You are the victor! You have won the war. Stir my soul to exult in You and rejoice in such a great salvation. Amen.

―❦―

When to Sing

> *"Is anyone among you suffering? Let him pray.*
> *Is anyone cheerful? Let him sing praise."*
> JAMES 5:13

Don't hold back! For fear of looking different or sounding bad, we can be tempted not to sing. Or we can be tempted to sing softly. If we are cheerful, we should sing! And we have so many reasons to be cheerful.

As we have studied together, there are numerous songs in Scripture that have even more reasons for us to be cheerful and sing. So, brothers, sing! Sing with all your soul. Be proud of the God who has saved you and rejoice in His great name. Join in with the saints who have gone before you and accompany the heavenly hosts singing praises to our God. He alone is worthy!

Dear God, Let me sing to You today of Your great love and kindness. Put a song in my heart and a melody on my tongue. Amen.

Strong Men

Defend

Samson's Story - His Birth

> *"for behold, you shall conceive and bear a son. No razor shall come upon his head, for the child shall be a Nazirite to God from the womb, and he shall begin to save Israel from the hand of the Philistines."*
> JUDGES 13:5

As we begin this section of our study of how to be men who are strong in the Lord, we're going to take note of certain men in Scripture who were defenders of God's people. First, we begin with Samson. Known for his incredible physical strength and his sacrificial death, he marvelously defended God's people.

It all began with a promise to his mom. She was told that he would be born and that he would need to take the Nazarite vow. In essence, this set him apart for God's use. As we seek to be men who are strong and defend what is right, we must make sure that we are doing so in line with God's word. We cannot make up rules and standards for ourselves and defend them in God's name. We must contend for the faith.

Dear God, teach me all there is to know from the life of Samson. Show me his failures and successes and give me wisdom. Amen.

⇒Day 180⇐

Samon's Story -
His Marriage

> *"His father and mother did not know that it was from the Lord, for he was seeking an opportunity against the Philistines. At that time the Philistines ruled over Israel."*
> JUDGES 14:4

As Samson grew up, God's people were at odds with the Philistines. There was such bitterness between the two people that war was just around the corner. Samson sought to marry one of the Philistine women. This confused his parents because it was common practice to marry from among your own people. However, Samson was doing this with a purpose. He was seeking an opportunity to fight for his people.

This Scripture is not teaching us to marry for a tactical advantage. But it teaches us that Samson's whole life, even down to who he chose to marry, was wed to this goal: to defend God's people. From his birth, through marriage, and unto death, this would be his goal. May we have this kind of commitment to upholding God's plan for our lives.

Dear God, I want all of my life to be used for Your glory. Lead me in the way You would have me to go. Amen.

Samson's Story – The Spirit of the Lord

"And the Spirit of the Lord rushed upon him, and he went down to Ashkelon and struck down thirty men of the town and took their spoil and gave the garments to those who had told the riddle. In hot anger he went back to his father's house."
JUDGES 14:19

This verse of Scripture is wrapped up where Samson's strength truly came from. All his successes were a gift of God. We see throughout the Bible that it is when the Spirit of the Lord comes over someone that miraculous things happen.

God was supplying everything Samson needed to accomplish his mission. He gave him the task from before his birth. He gave him a mother that would raise him in the right way. He gave him His Spirit and supernatural strength to accomplish it all. His whole life was an act of the grace of God. The same is true of us. Everything good that comes to us in life is a gracious gift from our heavenly Father.

Dear God, thank You for being so good to me. You have shown me grace upon grace. Amen.

Samson's Story - Unique Strategy

> *"So Samson went and caught 300 foxes and took torches. And he turned them tail to tail and put a torch between each pair of tails."*
> JUDGES 15:4

In this attack on the Philistine people, it's almost comical the strategy and ultimate success of Samson's efforts. Imagine sitting around the table discussing the best way to overcome an enemy city. Flaming foxes probably would not make your list of best ideas. But here we see God's provision and Samson's incredible strength again. He was able to catch 300 foxes. That's a tremendous feat. He then went on to tie those foxes together and put a torch between their tails. I'm not even sure how that is possible!

And yet God is providing for the man He has set to the task. He provided the opportunity, the fox-laden country, the torches, and the talent to pull it all off. Since God is the true defender of Israel, however, He sees fit to fight, He can. And He will always succeed.

Dear God, my defender and provider, please bless me in this way. Let all my efforts towards Your goals be successful. Amen.

Samson's Story - Incredible Strength

"And he found a fresh jawbone of a donkey, and put out his hand and took it, and with it he struck 1,000 men."
JUDGES 15:15

After inciting a riot by sending in the flaming foxes, the men of the city came out against Samsom. Being unprepared and making quick decisions that should not have worked, Samson found a jawbone from a donkey and put to death one thousand men.

This story is beginning to seem more and more ridiculous, but I hope we can see the point of it: God can and will use even the most meager of instruments for His goodwill. Maybe you're thinking to yourself that you're no Samson. There's nothing special about you. God doesn't have this fantastic call on your life to be the defender of His people. Think again. Was there anything special about a donkey's jawbone? No. The thing that makes anything special is when God decides to use it. God wants to use you.

Dear God, I want to be used by You. I admit that I don't know how or why You would use me, but I thank You for including me in Your mission. Amen.

Samson's Story - His Failure

> *"And the lords of the Philistines came up to her and said to her, "Seduce him, and see where his great strength lies, and by what means we may overpower him, that we may bind him to humble him. And we will each give you 1,100 pieces of silver."*
> JUDGES 16:5

There are a lot of good things to see in the life of Samson. He did some incredible things to fight for God's people. But, like all of the people God raised up to defend Israel, Samson was flawed. His arrogance and lust drove him into the arms of a woman named Delilah, who would betray him. She cut his hair, which broke his Nazarite vow to God, and he lost his strength.

We are all one bad decision away from weakness. None of us are above making that decision. We are all sinful and bent in that way. The only thing that separates the jawbone wielding Samson and captured one is the grace of God. Let's be diligent in thanking God for the grace He has shown us and ask that He would deliver us from evil.

❦

Dear God, I know that it is Your grace alone that has kept me from making a life-altering mistake. Keep me from such disaster. Amen.

❦

Samson's Story - His Redemption

"But the hair of his head began to grow again after it had been shaved."
JUDGES 16:22

For very few people, would this verse have the impact that it does Samson. His life was dedicated to serving God by defending His people. The sign of the vow that He made to God was physically represented by never cutting his hair. He broke that vow as he allowed himself to be seduced by Delilah. All he deserved after that moment was to be forgotten by God and punished.

Praise God, we don't always get what we deserve. He has stores of mercy ready for us. Where our sin increases, His mercy is more time and time again. You see, Samson's hair beginning to grow back was a picture of God's mercy and how He wasn't done with him yet. He hadn't forgotten about him.

Dear God, You have shown me so much mercy.
I do not deserve this relationship with You.
Help me to cherish it. Amen.

Samson's Story - His Defense

> *"And Samson said, "Let me die with the Philistines." Then he bowed with all his strength, and the house fell upon the lords and upon all the people who were in it. So the dead whom he killed at his death were more than those whom he had killed during his life."*
> JUDGES 16:30

Samson, battered, bruised, blind, and bald, cries out to God to be used by Him again. God allowed his hair to grow back and restored to him the mission he was on: to defend God's people. While chained to the auditorium's central pillars, with wonderful strength, Samson pulled with all of his might. And by the strength that God once again provided, he pulled the roof in on everyone inside. With his sacrifice, he placed a crucial blow on the Philistines.

Perhaps you have felt as if God is done with you. You have made a major mistake that has put you on the bench, and you feel like you'll never be restored. Don't lose heart. While we have to deal with our sin's effects in this life, God still desires to use you according to His purpose. Be patient and call out to God with sincerity of heart.

Dear God, I feel like Samson. I know I do not deserve to be used by You. I beg You to show mercy to me and give me a clear command to follow. Amen.

David's Mighty Men

> *"These are the names of the mighty men whom David had: Josheb-basshebeth a Tahchemonite; he was chief of the three. He wielded his spear against eight hundred whom he killed at one time."*
>
> 2 SAMUEL 23:8

King David surrounded himself with good men throughout his life. Before becoming king, he made a deep friendship with Jonathan. After being crowned, he had close friendships with people like Nathan. And now, towards the end of his reign, as people sought to kill him, he had a group of mighty men defended him. Let's take a few days to think about who those men were and why they were important.

With this introduction of the mighty men, I want us to see the need to link arms with someone worth protecting. This may be your wife, your family, a group of friends, or anyone who comes to mind. But there are people in your life that are worth fighting for. The challenge for us can be to determine who those people are. The Scripture makes it plain that we fight for our families and fight alongside faithful brothers and sisters.

Dear God, give me wisdom as I link arms with brothers to do Your work here on earth. Amen.

→ Day 188 ←

Defended by the Lord

> *"He rose and struck down the Philistines until his hand was weary, and his hand clung to the sword. And the Lord brought about a great victory that day, and the men returned after him only to strip the slain."*
> 2 SAMUEL 23:10

As we have seen throughout our study, the theme of the strength of His might is coming back up. While it was the man's weary hand that clung to the sword, it was the Lord that brought about a great victory. In this section describing the mighty men, we see the phrase come up over and over again.

Mysteriously, we work alongside God to accomplish His plans. He has not commissioned us to slay our enemies with swords. He has commissioned us to wield the sword of His word in the power of His Spirit to reach the nations with the gospel. Just as He did back then, He will bring about a great victory in our efforts.

Dear God, I am on a mission for You to share the gospel with the nations. I trust that You go before me in this endeavor. Amen.

Selfless Defense

> *"Then the three mighty men broke through the camp of the Philistines and drew water out of the well of Bethlehem that was by the gate and carried and brought it to David. But he would not drink of it. He poured it out to the Lord"*
> 2 SAMUEL 23:16

The men that surrounded David were selfless. He cried out for water during the battle. These mighty men broke into the enemy camp just to steal for him a canteen full of water. They put their lives on the line for such a small task.

This is the type of service we must give to King Jesus. Before ourselves, we must put Him. Whatever He desires, even if it means risking and losing our lives, we will do it in honor of the King. We must be selfless in our pursuit of this calling in our lives.

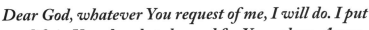

Dear God, whatever You request of me, I will do. I put my life in Your hands to be used for Your glory. Amen.

Team Defense

> *"He was the most renowned of the thirty and became their commander, but he did not attain to the three."*
> JUDGES 16:5

We cannot be strong and defend what God would have us to defend alone. We must surround ourselves with other people. David had over thirty mighty men that were working together. Those men not only needed David for direction, but they needed each other. Not everyone could be a leader. They had to trust one another and work together as a team.

The same is true for us as the Church, the body of Christ. We cannot all be the leader. We have different gifts given to us by God. So as we seek to be used by Him, let's be mindful of our teammates. Let's work together towards the goal of making disciples. We are not isolated or in competition with one another.

Dear God, You have given me teammates to work within the Church. Teach me to work with and not against this team. Amen.

The Battle of Jericho

> *"So the people shouted, and the trumpets were blown. As soon as the people heard the sound of the trumpet, the people shouted a great shout, and the wall fell down flat, so that the people went up into the city, every man straight before him, and they captured the city."*
> JOSHUA 6:20

The battle of Jericho is characterized by faith. Joshua is leading the nomadic Israelites into the Promised Land. God has said that He will give them into their hands if they follow a routine before waging war. They are to walk around the city walls silently for seven days. On the seventh day, they were to walk around and then end their walk with a mighty blast from their trumpets. With the roar of the horns, the walls fell down flat, and the war was won.

It takes faith to follow God. He will lead us into situations that we are unsure of. He will show us that He alone can do the impossible. He will do all these things for those who have placed their faith in Him. Ask yourself this today: who is my faith in?

Dear God, I confess that I place my faith in myself and in my abilities. Show me how to fully rely on You. Amen.

The Battle of Midian

> *"When they blew the 300 trumpets, the Lord set every man's sword against his comrade and against all the army. And the army fled as far as Beth-shittah toward Zererah, as far as the border of Abel-meholah, by Tabbath."*
> JUDGES 7:22

Gideon was the leader of God's people in this passage of Scripture. They have an interesting conversation before heading into battle. God tells him that his army is too big. He needs to cut thousands of people before heading into battle. This makes no sense in the eyes of a military leader. The bigger the army, the better, especially if you run the risk of being outnumbered. But there is no outnumbering God.

Through this battle plan, God displayed His strength and drew His people to trust Him. What has shaken your trust in God lately? What has made you second guess His plans for you? Keep His word firmly in mind when these doubts come. He has shown us time and time again that He is able to do abundantly more than we can think or ask.

Dear God, bolster me where my trust has been shaken. Remind me of Your word when Your plans do not make sense to me. I trust You. Amen.

The Battle of Amalek

> *"But Moses' hands grew weary, so they took a stone and put it under him, and he sat on it, while Aaron and Hur held up his hands, one on one side, and the other on the other side. So his hands were steady until the going down of the sun."*
> EXODUS 17:12

Defending is wearisome work. Let's take a moment to acknowledge the potential for burnout, weariness, and fatigue. Though we may have healthy minds and bodies, there is only so much that can be endured before we give way. There will be days when our hands are up, but we need to take a seat on solid rock.

If that's how you're feeling today, let me remind you of two things. The first is that we have a solid rock in Jesus Christ whom we can lean on in our time of need. And secondly, that we work in the strength of His might. It's not all up to us. It doesn't mean all ride on our efforts. We're laboring in the strength of His Spirit at the will of the Father.

Dear God, I am weary. I feel exhausted and ready to give up. Renew me with Your strength and teach me to lead on Your Son. Amen.

David and Goliath

> *"and that all this assembly may know that the Lord saves not with sword and spear. For the battle is the Lord's, and he will give you into our hand."*
> 1 SAMUEL 17:47

David and Goliath's story is so well known that it is commonly used by Christians and non-Christians alike to describe the underdog scenario. But this story is not just an underdog scenario. It is an impossible situation. Towering over David, Goliath was superior in strength, weaponry, and support. David had no chance.

But it wasn't dependent on David. He knew this. This is why, in his preparation to make his attack, he made the declaration that "the Lord saves not with sword and spear. . . He will give you into our hand." David's hope of success was riding on the capability of God to win the battle, not his own. Not only on God's capability to win but on God's desire to win for the sake of His people. This is our hope as well.

Dear God, You can do all things and desire to do good for Your people. Let that be my hope today. Amen.

Betrayal of Jesus

> *"And he came up to Jesus at once and said,*
> *"Greetings, Rabbi!" And he kissed him."*
> MATTHEW 26:49

Jesus is our true defender and greater example. Over the next few sections, we will take a long look at how His people's selfless defense led to His death. It all began with a kiss of betrayal from Judas. After spending roughly three years as His disciples, Judas decided to exchange his Lord for a few silver coins.

It was the beginning of a sadly ironic story. Jesus as the defender of His people, was being betrayed by them. Because of the actions of Judas, He would be put through an unjust trial, be mistreated along the way, and be hung on a cross to die. But by the sovereign design of our God, this is exactly the kind of defense His people needed. We needed Jesus to die in our place so that we can be seen in His place before God.

Dear God, how great a defense You have provided for me. Help me to see the depths of Your love as I study the final days of Jesus. Amen.

Unjust Trial of Jesus

"Now the chief priests and the whole council were seeking false testimony against Jesus that they might put him to death, but they found none, though many false witnesses came forward."
MATTHEW 26:59-60

I can remember one time in my life where I was falsely accused of something. A friend of mine had told our 8th-grade teacher that I had thrown a shoe at him during class. The accusation broke our relationship, and I had to pay the penalty for his false claims.

The chief priests were doing everything they could to have Jesus killed. They tried anything they could to make the accusation of blasphemy stick. They were ultimately successful in convincing those over Jesus' case that He was guilty of this. Jesus, however, did not sever His relationship with those who falsely accused. He ultimately used that accusation to repair their relationship with God.

Dear God, thank You for sending Jesus to restore our relationship. I do not deserve the kindness You have shown me. Amen.

Mistreatment of Jesus

> *"Then they spit in his face and struck him.*
> *And some slapped him"*
> MATTHEW 26:67

Following His unlawful trial, Jesus was beaten. Don't miss the significance of this. The man who they could find no one to give testimony against was at their mercy. Their goal was not just to have him tried or even killed. They wanted his final days to be painful. They were making a statement in their treatment of Him.

Jesus was making a statement as well. Without a single word spoken, His actions made clear His message. He was willfully suffering all of these things to accomplish His mission. May we be as dedicated to God's plan for us in our lives.

Dear God, Your Son endured heinous things at the hands of sinful men. Remind me that I was among them, and You saved me anyways. Amen.

Crucify Him

> *"Pilate said to them, "Then what shall I do with Jesus who is called Christ?" They all said, "Let him be crucified!"*
> MATTHEW 27:22

Pilate, unwilling to make the majority mad, offered up this option to the people. He said that he could release Barabbas, a proven murderer, and insurrectionist, or Jesus, a faultless man. The cry of the crowd is heartbreaking and only grew louder as Pilate tried to wash his hands of his guilt. Instead of their salvation, they chose guilt.

We have this same choice every day. We can rest in the salvation that Jesus offers or choose to cling to our guilt. If we are going to be strong men for the glory of God, we must not hold tightly to the chains that used to entangle us. Let's choose Christ today.

Dear God, Jesus has set me free! Teach me to live in the freedom that You offer. Amen.

Mocking of Jesus

> *"And they stripped him and put a scarlet robe on him, and twisting together a crown of thorns, they put it on his head and put a reed in his right hand. And kneeling before him, they mocked him, saying, "Hail, King of the Jews!""*
>
> MATTHEW 27:28-29

The depths of their depravity were on display as they mocked Jesus. They found enjoyment and pleasure in humiliating Jesus. Painfully, they dressed Him in taunting attire, doing their best to make Him feel the sting of their words.

I pray this isn't true, but maybe you have been in Jesus' shoes. Maybe you have endured the shameful mocking of enemies, or worse, friends. Let this suffering of our Lord be a comfort to you. He understands the pain you've gone through and more. He sees you, knows you, and loves you. He doesn't promise to take away the difficulty, but He does promise to see you through it.

Dear God, I'm sorry Your Son had to endure the humiliation He did for my sake. Thank You for walking with me through my pain. Amen.

⇒ Day 200 ⇐

The Irony of the Cross

> *"He saved others; he cannot save himself.*
> *He is the King of Israel; let him come down now*
> *from the cross, and we will believe in him."*
> MATTHEW 27:42

In a tragic irony, as Jesus hung on that tree, the people mocked Him all the more. They say He cannot save Himself and that if He did just that, they would believe. But it is because they won't believe that He continues to hang. Without His death on the cross, He would not save others in the way that they needed it the most.

See our Lord, nailed to the cross. He did this to save you. He had to be sacrificed in our place for our sin to save us in the most significant way. He endured the wrath of God so that we can enjoy His presence. I hope that we can appreciate and enjoy the irony of the cross.

Dear God, You have shown me so much love in sending Your Son. Because of Him, I can have salvation. Amen.

The Rejection on the Cross

> *"And about the ninth hour Jesus cried out with a loud voice, saying, "Eli, Eli, lema sabachthani?" that is, "My God, my God, why have you forsaken me?""*
> MATTHEW 28:46

In this whole process, the most painful moment of Jesus was not the betrayal from Judas, the beatings, mockings, or crown of thorns. It wasn't the nails driven through His hands or feet. It wasn't the difficult breaths He had to take by pulling Himself up on His pierced hands. None of that compares to the moment described in verse above. The Son felt the separation from the Father.

For all of eternity past, this was never a reality for Him. In perfect union with the Father and the Holy Spirit, there was never a hint of rejection. And yet, at this moment, Jesus felt the weight of this rejection in full force. He was beginning to experience the effects of becoming sin for our sake.

Dear God, I cannot imagine the pain You felt as you turned Your back on Your Son. I cannot fathom why He would choose to endure that for me. All I can say is, "Thank You." Amen.

The Death of Jesus

> *"And Jesus cried out again with a loud voice and yielded up his spirit."*
> MATTHEW 28:50

The Bible says that Jesus yielded up His spirit. There is wonderful significance to that phrase that we can rejoice in together. Even in the final moments of His life, Jesus was in full control. His life was not taken from Him. He is the King of all Creation. He is the master of life and death. If He was going to die, it would be at His own command. And for you and for me, He commanded it to be. He yielded His spirit to defend His people against the wrath of God.

The death of Jesus is our greatest hope in life. Not just because it happened, but how it happened and why. In the sovereign plan of God for His people, Jesus lived a perfect life and died a sacrificial death. Because of this, we can have eternal life.

Dear God, I praise You that You are in control of all things. The good and bad in life are all a part of Your plan. Help me to trust in You. Amen.

The Effect of the Cross

"And behold, the curtain of the temple was torn in two, from top to bottom. And the earth shook, and the rocks were split."
MATTHEW 28:51

In thunderous applause, all of the creation reacted to the death of our Lord. While humanity saw destruction, Jesus was accomplishing reconciliation. The curtain torn in the temple was in between the inner sanctuary and the holy of holies. This was a place that only the High Priest got to enter to commune with God.

The tearing of the curtain from top to bottom was God's way of expressing what He had done. Through the death of His Son, He broke through to commune with His people. So, let's join in with all creation. Let's lift our voices to sing of the victory accomplished for us at the cross. Let's embrace the gift of being able to have a relationship with our God.

Dear God, it is such a privilege to talk with You. Help me to not take it for granted. Amen.

The Defense of the Cross

"When the centurion and those who were with him, keeping watch over Jesus, saw the earthquake and what took place, they were filled with awe and said, "Truly this was the Son of God!""
MATTHEW 28:54

This is the point! Jesus' death on the cross was not meant to be considered in isolation. It was meant to change the world. More specifically, it was meant to change the hearts of the world. Having seen what he has done, the centurion cries out in awe. With a bloodied spear in his hand, he sees the significance of the death of Jesus.

Take some time to ask God for this kind of clarity. Ask Him to open your eyes to the significance of the cross. Ask Him to change your world by changing Your heart. It's this kind of result that He was after sending His Son to die in the first place.

Dear God, open my eyes to the significance of the cross. Change my heart and help me to see all You've done. Amen.

Peter Defends Jesus

> *"And behold, one of those who were with Jesus stretched out his hand and drew his sword and struck the servant of the high priest and cut off his ear."*
> MATTHEW 26:51

In our efforts to defend, with the right motives, we may end up with wrong methods. Peter was in the garden the night that Jesus was arrested. After the betraying kiss of Judas, the soldiers who accompanied him went to arrest Jesus. Peter reached for the dagger at his side and lunged to Jesus' defense. He cut the ear off of his opponent.

Jesus, overflowing with grace and mercy, picked the man's ear up and placed it back on the soldier's head. Peter's desire to defend was not wrong. Jesus' desire to do the will of His Father was just a higher calling. In our efforts, let's make sure to keep the will of God at its rightful place: our highest priority.

Dear God, in my zeal to do what is right, I can overlook my highest aim: the glory of Your name. Teach me to stay focused. Amen.

Reuben Defends Joseph

> *"But when Reuben heard it, he rescued him out of their hands, saying, "Let us not take his life."*
> GENESIS 37:21

Joseph was the favorite son among his twelve brothers. His father obviously favored him, and it drove his brothers to anger. While they were out shepherding their flocks, they formed a plan to get rid of Joseph. They were going to kill him. Reuben stepped in but didn't step up. He suggested that they throw him into a pit and sell him into slavery. That's better than having him killed, but it wasn't the fullest version of good.

Brothers, we're going to be faced with opportunities to step in and step up. We must push for the fullest version of good, not just a not-as-bad alternative. Don't halfway do your job. Fight for the good of others, even if it puts you on the outside.

Dear God, help me to discern between right and wrong. Give me the boldness to stand up for those who need help. Amen.

Abraham Defends His Wife

> *"Abraham said, "I did it because I thought,*
> *'There is no fear of God at all in this place,*
> *and they will kill me because of my wife."*
>
> GENESIS 20:11

Abraham was a lot of things. He was a shepherd. He was the father of the nation of Israel. He was someone who was counted righteous because of his faith. He was obedient to a God who called him to leave his home to journey to a new land. But he was also a liar. Two times, he lied to foreign kings about his wife. He would say that she was his sister so that they wouldn't harm her or him. Both times, he was caught in his sin.

We're going to make mistakes. In fact, we're going to make the same mistakes, even after being caught red-handed. This is why we so desperately need the mercy of Jesus in our everyday life. Although we strive for holiness, we will never reach perfection while we're alive.

Dear God, I am prone to make the same mistakes
over and over again. Let Your mercy be new
every morning. Amen.

Abraham Defends Lot

> *"Then he said, "Oh let not the Lord be angry, and I will speak again but this once. Suppose ten are found there." He answered, "For the sake of ten I will not destroy it.""*
>
> GENESIS 18:32

In this passage, Abraham pleads to God to reconsider his judgment on Sodom. The town was full of wickedness and wicked people. It was also home to a member of Abraham's family, Lot. Abraham prayed to God, asking Him to spare the city if there were just a few righteous people who love Him within its limits. The terrible part of the story is that Lot was not righteous himself.

God knew this. He also knew that Abraham would barter to protect the life of his family. God, sovereign over both means and ends in life, mercifully let this play out to grow the faith of Abraham and open the eyes of Lot. Plead with God with the desires of your heart and trust that He will give whatever is best for you.

Dear God, I trust You with my life. You have been faithful to do what is for my good and Your glory. Amen.

Strong Men

Serve

Freedom to Serve

> *"For you were called to freedom, brothers.*
> *Only do not use your freedom as an opportunity*
> *for the flesh, but through love serve one another."*
> GALATIANS 5:13

We have a choice to make. Through His atoning death on the cross, Christ has set us free from the bondage of sin. We are no longer bound. By the power of the Spirit, we can live righteous lives. We do not have to fear the penalty of sin because it has been paid for on the cross. The choice we have to make now is how we will live?

Will we live in a way that takes advantage of freedom? Will we continue to pursue sin knowing that our debt has been paid? Or will we live in freedom to serve one another? Paul's encouragement to the Galatian church is to live to serve one another. Take a moment to examine your life and see how you are choosing to live in freedom.

Dear God, You have freed me from the penalty of sin.
Lead me in the way of freedom that lives to serve. Amen.

He Came to Serve

> *"For even the Son of Man came not to be served but to serve, and to give his life as a ransom for many."*
> MARK 10:45

Jesus came to serve. This is a mind-blowing thought when we consider the greatness of King Jesus. He is the omnipotent ruler of all things, and He chose to serve His people by sacrificing Himself for them. If this is our King's position, how can we choose to live in any other way?

There are countless ways to serve others around us. We can give our time, our money, or our abilities. We can do the grocery shopping for a widow or single mother. We can sit down and talk with a friend who is going through a hard time. We can teach a young man how to change his oil. Whatever it may be, find a way to serve your neighbor in a way that points them to Jesus.

Dear God, open my eyes to opportunities to serve my neighbor today. Amen.

Gifted to Serve

> *"As each has received a gift, use it to serve one another,
> as good stewards of God's varied grace."*
> 1 PETER 4:10

Everyone is good or passionate about something. Sometimes these passions are particularly useful, like auto mechanics, accounting, public speaking. Sometimes, these passions are more for entertainment purposes like sports, comics, or movies. Whatever your skillset or passions, they are to be used for the sake of the kingdom. We are to serve one another with our gifts.

Take some time today to pinpoint where you are gifted or what you're passionate about. Then think about how you can use those things to build gospel relationships or do kingdom work. Be creative! The Bible tells us to use our gifts but gives us the freedom to see how best to do so.

*Dear God, You have specifically given me passions
and giftings for a purpose. Show me what
that purpose is. Amen.*

Servant of All

> *"And he sat down and called the twelve.*
> *And he said to them, "If anyone would be first,*
> *he must be last of all and servant of all."*
> MARK 9:35

What Jesus is describing here is not a position but a posture. It is how we view ourselves in light of what Jesus has done for us. Since He has served us by sacrificing His life for us, our daily posture ought to serve others.

It takes serious heart surgery to humble ourselves to this place in life. We naturally desire to be served. It is our aim to put ourselves ahead of others and seek our own good first. A posture of service does the exact opposite. This is why we need the tremendous help of the Holy Spirit to get to that spiritual place.

Dear God, I desire to be a servant to all, but I struggle with my sinful desires of selfishness. Rid me of my sinful ways. Amen.

A Following Servant

> *"If anyone serves me, he must follow me; and where I am, there will my servant be also. If anyone serves me, the Father will honor him."*
> JOHN 12:26

Because it is against our nature to want to serve others, we have to be taught how to serve. This means that it takes work to grow in this area. It means that we have to spend time following Jesus by reading His word, watching faithful saints do it in front of us, asking our brothers and sisters for help or feedback as we learn.

We have to begin to be intentional with our lives if we are going to be servants in the way that Jesus shows us in His word. Maybe what you need to do is a block of a portion of your day or week for the sake of pursuing this path. Skip an episode of your favorite show and read a chapter in a good book on the subject. Instead of eating lunch alone, eat it with a good friend who is doing this well. Learn from one another.

Dear God, help me to reorientate my life around the goal of service. Teach me to be intentional in all that I do. Amen.

A Following Servant

> *" but emptied himself, by taking the form of a servant,*
> *being born in the likeness of men."*
> PHILIPPIANS 2:7

Theologians have spilled a lot of ink arguing over what it means for Jesus to have emptied Himself. There are a few things we know for sure it did not mean. It does not mean that He became less godly. It does not mean that He was no longer able to do whatever He willed. It does mean that He took a different approach when descending from heaven to be born on earth as a baby boy.

In essence, He willfully gave up certain rights as God to serve His people in a way that would save them. We don't have the same rights as Him to give up, but we do have the opportunity to empty ourselves for other people. Although we may have the right to act or react in a certain way, could we serve our neighbors better if we gave up our rights at times?

Dear God, give me discernment and wisdom. I want to serve my neighbor well. Help me to think through what it would mean to give up certain rights to do so. Amen.

A Family Value

> *"And if it is evil in your eyes to serve the Lord, choose this day whom you will serve, whether the gods your fathers served in the region beyond the River, or the gods of the Amorites in whose land you dwell. But as for me and my house, we will serve the Lord."*
>
> JOSHUA 24:15

What are some of the things that make your family unique? Maybe you're marked by a love for a certain collegiate team. Perhaps you're the family that is always first or last to a gathering. Or maybe you're marked by a bigger, deeper idea. My family is marked by adoption. We adopted our son when he was 4 years old and are big proponents of adoption and foster care. It is a family value for us.

When we think about what it means to be servants, it becomes a family value for us. We should strive to be known as the family that is always willing to serve. This will exemplify that behavior in front of /with your children a key in making this happen.

Dear God, as for my family and me, we will serve You. Empower us to do this, I pray. Amen.

Jesus Serves You

> *"For who is the greater, one who reclines at table or one who serves? Is it not the one who reclines at table? But I am among you as the one who serves."*
> LUKE 22:27

We have talked about how Jesus came as a servant for all, but I want us to concentrate for a moment on how Jesus came to serve you. Yes, you. There is a corporate aspect to Jesus' mission. He came to seek and save a people, but He also came to seek and save you. There is an intimacy and particular care that I don't want us to miss.

We are loved by Jesus personally. He came with the intent to serve us each as individuals and not as a part of some corporate program. We, too, should practice this kind of service. It's less about how many people I can serve in the most efficient way possible and more about how I can serve individuals in the most loving way possible.

Dear God. I want to be personal and intimate in my service to other people. I want them to feel the warmth of Your love as I do this. Amen.

Do the Dirty Work

> *"If I then, your Lord and Teacher, have washed your feet,*
> *you also ought to wash one another's feet."*
> JOHN 13:14

Washing someone's feet is one of the most disgusting tasks I can think of. And if we take a moment to consider these statements' cultural background, we will find it even more off-putting. These men had been walking on dusty roads in sandals. The streets contained garbage, animal feces, mud, and more. To wash someone's feet was the responsibility of the lowest servant. This is what Jesus did for His disciples and what He did for us on the cross. He washed the dirtiest parts of our souls with His shed blood. If this is true for us, how much more should we not shy away from the dirty work of serving others. Whether physically dirty, emotionally sticky, or spiritually challenging, let's get our hands dirty.

Dear God, sign me up for the dirty work. You have washed me white as snow. Let that be my motivation in my service to others. Amen.

Serve the Lord

"Only fear the Lord and serve him faithfully with all your heart. For consider what great things he has done for you."
1 SAMUEL 12:24

As a musician, I put my whole heart into my music. It moves every part of me. My physical body, emotional state, and spiritual posture are all affected by the songs I lead and sing at church. I serve in that way with my whole heart.

The Bible teaches us to serve the Lord with all of our hearts. We are to commit to serving Him with everything that we have and all that we are. Take inventory of your life. What is being used for His service, and what is still set off to the side for you to use personally. Challenge yourself today to give it all over to Him.

Dear God, dig into my life and peer into my deepest closets. Find the stores of things I am keeping for myself and claim them for Your use. Amen.

A New Way to Serve

> *"But now we are released from the law, having died to that which held us captive, so that we serve in the new way of the Spirit and not in the old way of the written code."*
> ROMANS 7:6

Before Jesus' work on the cross, God's people served Him by following the ceremonial and sacrificial laws. There were hundreds of them to follow. We can get a glimpse into that world when we read the book of Leviticus. But now, because Christ has fulfilled the law in His life and death, we no longer are under the Mosaic Law. We are now to walk in the way of the Spirit.

The way of the Spirit still has at its core the moral laws like the ones found in the Ten Commandments, but it is more focused on following the examples of Christ and the teachings of His apostles in the New Testament. Let's dig in and learn this new way of service together.

Dear God, Your Son has fulfilled the requirements of the old law. Teach me how to live in the new of the Spirit. Amen.

Serving Jesus

"And the King will answer them, 'Truly, I say to you, as you did it to one of the least of these my brothers, you did it to me."
MATTHEW 25:40

If you really want to serve a parent, serve their children. Love them. Offer to watch them if the need arises. Be a kind and safe face for them to see when they see you. This kind of service to the children serves the parents as well. Jesus teaches in the book of Matthew that when we serve "the least of these," then we're serving Him too.

It's not that we are literally serving Him. We are spiritually serving Him because He has given us this command. We are loving His children and, in turn, loving Him. Let's keep an eye out for the least of these among us. Let's look for opportunities to serve them and ultimately serve our Lord.

Dear God, Your Son became the least of these for me. I want to serve Him by serving others around me. Amen.

⇛ Day 221 ⇚

Servant Leadership

> *"For what we proclaim is not ourselves, but Jesus Christ as Lord, with ourselves as your servants for Jesus' sake."*
> 2 CORINTHIANS 4:5

Paul and his co-laborers mentioned in this passage were involved in the church's leadership at Corinth. While Paul was not a pastor at that church, he played an instrumental role in its foundation and growth. The way that the leadership at Corinth was operating was with their eye towards service.

If you're in leadership at your local church or in leadership in another facet of your life, do you have your eye towards service? Are you leading by serving others for Jesus' sake? These are good questions to ponder as we evaluate how we lead. Ask the Holy Spirit to give you insight into your own heart so that you can see it clearly.

Dear God, I want to be a servant leader like Your Son is for His people. Serve me by showing me where I can grow in this area. Amen.

Well, Done

> *"His master said to him, 'Well done, good and faithful servant. You have been faithful over a little; I will set you over much. Enter into the joy of your master.'"*
> MATTHEW 25:21

These are the words that I long to hear one day from my Master. In fact, there may not be sweeter words to my ears than the validation that I have done my job well. As we work hard to serve others, let's keep this goal in mind: When we finish the work, we will receive validation and joy from our Master.

We don't have to wait to get a taste of those things. We can read His word and see page after page of joy. It overflows from the binding of the book and into our hearts. Let this joy now and the fuller joy to come fuel our service to Him.

Dear God, I look forward to the day when You will say, "Well done, good and faithful servant." Make me worthy of that remark. Amen.

⇒ Day 223 ⇐

Serve the Poor

*"Whoever is generous to the poor lends to the Lord,
and he will repay him for his deed."*
PROVERBS 19:17

While we serve all people, God has a special heart for the poor, orphaned, widowed, and foreigners. He sees them as people in special need of help. As His hand and feet, we are to go and meet that need in whatever way we can. Like we say with how Jesus spoke about it, giving to the poor is like giving to the Lord.

What a privilege that is in and of itself. But God being abundant in grace, says that if we are generous to the poor, we will be repaid for our deeds. This isn't a tax break or a promise of prosperity. However, in whatever way He will, God promises to bless those who bless others out of their abundance. Let's be a blessing today.

*Dear God, You have blessed me and given me
all that I need. Give me the opportunity
to bless someone else. Amen.*

Bless and Be Blessed

*"Whoever brings blessing will be enriched,
and one who waters will himself be watered."*
PROVERBS 11:25

This concept is found throughout the Bible, that if we bless others, we will be blessed. Let's take a moment to think about how this plays out. Is it a dollar-for-dollar trade-off? Are blessings limited to financial or physical value? What does it even mean to be blessed?

Let me give you a large framework to work in. To be blessed means to have the favor of God shown to you. That could be financial, physical, health-related, etc. But there is a deeper and greater blessing that is a sure promise for us, that is, Jesus Christ. He is the true way to have a favor with God. So while God may bless in other ways, the sure blessing we receive when blessing others is a deeper relationship with our Lord.

Dear God, You have blessed me and put me in a position to bless others. Press me forward in giving to others as I can. Amen.

Working Faith

> *"and one of you says to them, "Go in peace, be warmed and filled," without giving them the things needed for the body, what good is that?"*
> JAMES 2:16

James hits us with a challenging thought in this passage of Scripture. He is detailing for us the relationship between faith and works. He brings up this example. What if we see someone in the street that is hungry and in need of food? What does a person of faith do in that situation? Some may say that you can just simply pray for them. James argues that praying that they would be filled and actually giving them something to fill them are entirely different signs of faith.

James is not anti-prayer, but he is anti-excuse. Frequently when immediate physical needs are present, the believer can meet those needs. We need to push ourselves to act in faith, letting our works prove it to be genuine.

Dear God, I admit that it is much easier for me to say I will pray for someone to physically help. Embolden me to live out my faith. Amen.

Pure Religion

> *"Religion that is pure and undefiled before God the Father is this: to visit orphans and widows in their affliction and to keep oneself unstained from the world."*
> JAMES 1:27

According to James, there are two marks of genuine Christianity. The first is that we would serve the marginalized in our society. For James, those were the orphans and the widows. Today, those people groups may vary, but they are still there. The second is that we would pursue holiness.

It is clear that visiting the orphans and the widows is service, but how is our holiness a service to others? Our holiness is a witness to others and shows them the power of the Gospel. We are not any better than them. The only thing that separates us from them is the grace of God, and that grace is freely available to all. Let's pursue pure and undefiled religion before God.

Dear God, instill in me a passion for caring for the marginalized and pursuing holiness. I do this all by Your grace. Amen.

Neglecting Good

> " *Do not neglect to do good and to share what you have,
> for such sacrifices are pleasing to God.*"
> HEBREWS 13:16

The command not to neglect to do good is hitting at a subtle sin issue in our lives. It's one thing to reject the option to do good. It's another thing to neglect. Imagine seeing someone drowning in a pool. Choosing not to attempt to save them would be despicable. But what about the person that walks by without noticing the cries for help because they are too distracted with whatever is on their mind? The same result happens either way: death.

Brother, the author of Hebrews, is pushing us to be diligent in our pursuit of doing good. Our trouble usually isn't the denial of good actions. It's neglecting to do them because we are distracted by our own desires and thoughts.

Dear God, tune my ears to hear the subtle cries for help from those in my life. Take away the distractions that clog my vision. Amen.

Good Will Service

> *"rendering service with a good will*
> *as to the Lord and not to man,"*
> EPHESIANS 6:7

Our attitude matters. Don't believe me? Go on a date with your wife with a bitter disposition the whole time and see how that goes. She will let you know quickly that your attitude matters. Here, in Paul's letter to the church in Ephesus. He addresses the matter of our attitude in our service to others.

He says that we are to serve with goodwill. This means that we are to serve with an attitude of friendliness or helpfulness. It means that when we pray for someone, we don't harbor judgmental thoughts. It means that when we teach a class for the church, we don't stroke our own pride. Our attitude matters. We ought to be mindful of what's going on in our minds.

Dear God, You know my every thought and intention. Purify my motives as I seek to serve. Amen.

The Common Service

> *"Bear one another's burdens,*
> *and so fulfill the law of Christ."*
> GALATIANS 6:2

This is probably one of the most common and meaningful ways to serve our brothers and sisters in Christ. Not everyone has a financial strain, a lack of food or clothing, or car troubles. But everyone has burdens. We live in a sin-wrecked world among sinful people. Burdens are a natural part of life.

What is unnatural is for people to seek to share our burdens. What a relief we can offer to others if we will simply genuinely ask how they are doing. Don't settle for "good" or "fine." Ask them again and see if their answer changes. Sometimes, when people are given a chance to stop and think about the question, they realize they are ready to talk with someone about it. Be ready for those opportunities to bear those burdens.

Dear God, my brothers, and sisters are burdened
from life. Put me in their paths so that
I can help to bear the load. Amen.

Serve the Household of Faith

> *"So then, as we have opportunity,*
> *let us do good to everyone, and especially*
> *to those who are of the household of faith."*
> GALATIANS 6:10

We have a hierarchy of responsibility in our lives. We are to love God, first, our wives second, and so on, depending on your family situation. In the world of service, there is a hierarchy as well. Paul tells the Galatian church that they are to do good to everyone, especially the household of faith.

Let me pose this question to you: when you serve, do you have special attention given to your brothers and sisters in Christ? When we choose to especially do good to them, we have a ripple effect that better serves the greater majority. It's a similar thought to the emergency protocol on an airplane. When air masks are deployed, we put one on ourselves before turning to help another. Let's keep our mask on while we help others.

Dear God, You have given me the great gift of a family in my church body. Use me to care for them so we can better care for the dying world. Amen.

Simple Service

> *"not neglecting to meet together, as is the habit of some, but encouraging one another, and all the more as you see the Day drawing near."*
> HEBREWS 10:25

Maybe you're reading this section on service, and you're ready to get to work but do not know where to begin. Let me set the bar low and fan into flame the desire that is growing in you. The simplest way you can serve your church family is to gather with them and encourage them. Just be there and let them know you're there for them.

A smiling face across the sanctuary and a warm greeting goes a long way. When we offer a prayer for our brothers going through a difficult time or asking about a sister who had an exciting opportunity come up, we give encouragement to a body that needs it. Be there and let them know you're there for them.

Dear God, I want to be there for my church family. Help me to be present in every sense of the word. Amen.

Appointed by Christ

> *"I thank him who has given me strength,*
> *Christ Jesus our Lord, because he judged me faithful,*
> *appointing me to his service,"*
> 1 TIMOTHY 1:12

When I was in elementary school, we had a school government that we could be a part of. To be in the government, you had to be elected to a certain position. I decided one year that I was going to run for Treasurer. I had no idea what I was signing up for, but I wanted to be involved with what was going on. I remember getting elected and feeling the weight of being appointed to the task.

Jesus has appointed us to the task of serving Him. Like me in elementary school, there are many times where we don't exactly know what all that means. But it's good for us to feel the weight of that calling from time to time so that we can remember who it is that called us.

Dear God, You have appointed me to Your service. Allow me to feel the magnitude of being appointed by my Creator this week. Amen.

Life-Changing Service

> *"if you pour yourself out for the hungry and satisfy the desire of the afflicted, then shall your light rise in the darkness and your gloom be as the noonday."*
> ISAIAH 58:10

Some of us will get the unique opportunity to serve someone in a way that truly changes their lives. I have been served in this way a handful of times. It's a service that gets to truly satisfy the one in need. It brings light into their darkness. It changes their gloom to the bright hope of noonday.

With the gospel message, we can offer this life-changing service to everyone we meet. Jesus is the light of the world. Jesus is the only one who can satisfy. Jesus is the only true joy there is to be had. Let's share His story with the world and take advantage of the rare opportunities to change someone's life forever.

Dear God, I have been served in ways that have drastically changed my life. Use me as an agent to provide that kind of change to someone in my life. Amen.

Excellent Service

"So he left all that he had in Joseph's charge, and because of him he had no concern about anything but the food he ate."
GENESIS 39:6

The life of Joseph is filled with drama, as we have discussed in past devotions. One of the consistent themes that we see in Joseph's life is that he is found serving someone with excellence wherever he is. His service was seen as so excellent by both Potiphar in this passage and Pharaoh that he is given command over nearly everything.

This is the kind of service that we ought to offer others. We need to strive to serve with excellence, no matter how small the task. If the most we can do for someone is to scrub their toilets, let's make them shine. This is seen by both men and God and oftentimes rewarded. But greater than that, it is a testimony of the excellent work done for us in Christ Jesus.

Dear God, when people see my efforts, I pray that they will find excellence. To the glory of Your name, empower me to be excellent. Amen.

Hold Them Up

> *"But Moses' hands grew weary, so they took a stone and put it under him, and he sat on it, while Aaron and Hur held up his hands, one on one side, and the other on the other side. So his hands were steady until the going down of the sun."*
> Exodus 17:12

In God's mysterious, sovereign plan, for the Israelites to prevail against their enemies, Moses had to hold his staff in the air. Battles lasted a long time, and naturally, Moses' arms became tired. As his staff was lowered, Israel began to fall back and lose. When his staff was raised again, they would begin to prevail. Seeing this, Aaron and Hur came up to help Moses. They helped him to hold his arms up so that his people would prevail.

Sometimes, the most meaningful thing you can do for the kingdom is to hold up someone's arms. You won't be remembered for holding the staff. People won't look back and talk about how you saved certain people. But without someone to hold his arms, Moses would have failed. Whatever position God has called you to serve in, know that it plays a vital role.

Dear God, there is purpose in my service. Help me not to seek acknowledgment from men, but trust that You see all that I do. Amen.

Lent to the Lord

*"Therefore I have lent him to the Lord.
As long as he lives, he is lent to the Lord."*
1 SAMUEL 1:28

Samuel's mom, Hannah, was barren. She prayed earnestly that God would give her a son. She promised that if He gave her a son, she would dedicate him to serve the Lord in His temple. God was gracious and granted her request with her baby boy, Samuel. When it came time for him to be given over, Hannah kept her promise and lent him to the Lord.

Unknown to Samuel for part of his life, there were tearful prayers offered up for his sake. This is often true of us, and we don't even know. There are people who have spent hours praying for us. Whether our parents, grandparents, future spouses, or church families, prayers have been offered up for you. God has heard and answered many of those prayers, and here you are, ready to serve at His pleasure. Let's get to work.

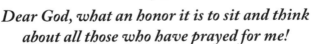

*Dear God, what an honor it is to sit and think
about all those who have prayed for me!
Use me how You will. Amen.*

Send Me

> *"And I heard the voice of the Lord saying,*
> *"Whom shall I send, and who will go for us?"*
> *Then I said, "Here I am! Send me."*
> ISAIAH 6:8

I played football one year in high school. It was terrifying. I had a love for the game that grew from watching the NFL for years with my brothers and dad, but when it came to actually play football, I was horrified. Standing at an intimidating five foot four inches and a whopping one hundred pounds, I was not striking fear into anyone's hearts. One day, Coach called my number and told me to get in the game. And off I went to do my best and hope to survive.

Our number has been called. God has called to His people, "Whom will I send?" He is looking at the bench, and He has locked eyes with you. Will you say, "Here I am! Send me?" Tighten your pads and put your helmet on. It's time to get in the game.

Dear God, I'm scared of what it may mean,
but here I am. Send me. Amen.

Reluctant Service

> *"But Jonah rose to flee to Tarshish from the presence of the Lord. He went down to Joppa and found a ship going to Tarshish. So he paid the fare and went down into it, to go with them to Tarshish, away from the presence of the Lord."*
> JONAH 1:3

The temptation to run will be present with every opportunity to serve someone. Jonah fell to that temptation when he was called by God to go and preach to the nation of Nineveh. In his defense, Nineveh was a wicked place that was likely to try to kill him for preaching such a message. Nevertheless, this was his assignment, and he ran. Ultimately God pulled him back in, and he did what he was called to do.

Let's not waste time running. It only causes pain and heartache for us. Nothing will stop the plan of God. If He has called you to a purpose, then it will come to pass. Whether we go through it fighting tooth and nail or joyfully is up to us. Let's choose joyful obedience today, not reluctant service.

Dear God, I confess that I have been reluctant to serve You in different ways. Show me the joy of obedience. Amen.

Strong Men
Lead

We are Leaders

"Come, I will send you to Pharaoh that you may bring my people, the children of Israel, out of Egypt."
EXODUS 3:10

We are all leaders in some way. Some of us lead in our churches. Others lead on our job sites. Still more lead their families. And some lead friends. We are all tasked with the responsibility of leading someone. Let's be sure that we are leading well.

Over the next few devotions, we will take time to look at Moses' call to lead God's people out of Egypt. Moses was one of the most influential leaders to ever have the position among God's people, but it started off in a rocky way. We will listen and learn from his mistakes together.

Dear God, You use me as a leader in different ways in my life. Work in me to make me a worthy leader. Amen.

Who Am I?

> *"But Moses said to God, "Who am I that I should go to Pharaoh and bring the children of Israel out of Egypt?"*
> EXODUS 3:11

When faced with the opportunity to lead, we will eventually have to wrestle with the question, "Who am I?" What makes me good enough to be followed? Who would want to follow someone like me? Implicit in these questions, there is a stroke of humility that is healthy.

What I want us to see is the lack of faith in these questions. As leaders, we have been appointed by God to our various tasks. There's a sense in which it doesn't matter who you are. Your name has been called by someone far greater than you are. Trust in the One who has called you and not yourself as you step into your leadership role.

Dear God, who am I that I would be given the opportunity to lead? Help me wrap my mind around that my calling is more important to consider than my abilities. Amen.

God with Us

"He said, "But I will be with you, and this shall be the sign for you, that I have sent you: when you have brought the people out of Egypt, you shall serve God on this mountain."
EXODUS 3:12

In response to Moses' question, "Who am I?" God answers, "It's not about you, It's about Me. I will be with you." This is our great comfort and boldness as we lead. God goes with us. He goes to protect, guide, and strengthen us as we face the challenges of leadership. We will never be alone, even when we feel isolated.

For a few moments together, we ought to take time to appreciate the presence of God when difficult circumstances come our way. He hasn't left us to figure it out ourselves. When they come, let's lean on His leadership, the one who knows the beginning and the end of our journey.

Dear God, thank You for always being with me. I feel lost and alone at times. Reveal Your presence to me. Amen.

What If . . .

> *"Then Moses answered, "But behold, they will not believe me or listen to my voice, for they will say, " 'The Lord did not appear to you."*
> EXODUS 4:1

Are you the type of person to run all of the "what if" scenarios in your head? Do you calculate every possible outcome and strategize around every possible challenge? In short, do you overthink things? There is value in being thoughtful and having genuine concern. However, when those concerns paralyze us, we have fallen into disobedience and not prudence.

Praise God that He doesn't get fed up with us and leave us in a paralyzed state. Graciously, He walks with us through our concerns and leads us towards action. Share your concerns with your heavenly Father. Don't allow them to shackle your actions.

Dear God, I'm worried about what my future holds and the plans You have for me. Help me to walk in faith. Amen.

I'm Not Able

> *"But Moses said to the Lord, "Oh, my Lord, I am not eloquent, either in the past or since you have spoken to your servant, but I am slow of speech and of tongue."*
> EXODUS 4:10

Moses' calling was to lead God's people out of Egypt and into the Promised Land. A necessary step in all of this was to have a hard conversation with Pharoah and convince Israel that he was really the appointed leader. Therefore, his concern about not being the best speaker makes sense. However, God doesn't allow Moses' inability to stop him.

Nothing will thwart the plan of God. Moses' inability did not surprise God, and neither does ours. He knows exactly what He is getting when He calls us to lead. He is getting an opportunity for His glory to shine through our weakness. He is getting a chance to display His strength. We shouldn't shy away from those opportunities.

Dear God, let Your glory shine through in my weakness. Use me despite my shortcomings. Amen.

Never Lead Alone

> *"And Moses told Aaron all the words of the Lord with which he had sent him to speak, and all the signs that he had commanded him to do."*
> EXODUS 4:28

God is abundant in His grace to us. He not only promises to personally be with us as we figure out how to lead, but He also provides faithful brothers that we can walk alongside. For Moses, He gave Aaron to help with his struggle with speaking. Aaron became a sort of mouthpiece for Moses.

Brother, link arms with someone. Walk through this life and figure things out together. Don't waste time acting like you have it all together. That doesn't do you or anyone else any good. Lean into grace. Accept your weakness. Reach out for help. You'll be surprised how you will be able to help those who are helping you.

Dear God, You are so good to me. You have given me brothers that can help me in this life. Draw us together and let iron sharpen iron. Amen.

Difficult Leadership

> *"Let heavier work be laid on the men that they may labor at it and pay no regard to lying words."*
> EXODUS 5:9

Good leadership doesn't always mean that life is easy for everyone. Moses led God's people exactly as he was supposed to, which led to hardship, plagues, and the death of many children in Egypt. Good leadership doesn't shy away from hard times. It seeks to lead well through them and allow God to do refining work in the process.

If you're in the midst of a hard leadership season, look for the growth opportunities that are there for you. How is God using this to cause you to trust Him more? Is this situation giving you a sharper sense of how to love people that are different from you? Hard times don't mean bad leadership. It's an opportunity to be a better leader.

Dear God, help me to learn as I lead through this difficult season. Refine me like gold in the fire. Amen.

Lead by God

> *"And the Lord went before them by day in a pillar of cloud to lead them along the way, and by night in a pillar of fire to give them light, that they might travel by day and by night."*
> EXODUS 13:21

After these difficult conversations with Pharaoh and the 10 plagues resulting in the death of every firstborn male child in Egypt, Moses leads God's people out. God personally leads His people out of bondage and towards the Promised Land. He manifests Himself as a pillar of cloud by day and a pillar of fire by night. Can you imagine such an amazing sight?

Here we see a clear picture of godly leadership. It is not about how wise and influential Moses can be. We know that he was not. And it's not about how bold and courageously he could speak the truth. He didn't want to do that either. It's about being a leader that follows God. Moses wasn't being innovative or coming up with a plan as he went along. He was simply following God's lead. That's our job as well.

Dear God, I want to follow Your leadership.
Make the path clear for me. Amen.

Delegation

> *"Moreover, look for able men from all the people, men who fear God, who are trustworthy and hate a bribe, and place such men over the people as chiefs of thousands, of hundreds, of fifties, and of tens."*
> EXODUS 18:21

Not too long after Moses led God's people out of Egypt, he realized the difficulty of the task before him. He has thousands and thousands of people to lead. This means that he had thousands and thousands of issues to handle. Remember, God's people weren't perfect. Along the way, there were disputes among many of the people, and Moses was the one who had to settle them. It was exhausting.

Jethro stepped in and gave Moses some much-needed advice. He suggested that Moses delegate his responsibilities. He said to give the smaller matters to another group of individuals and let the bigger matters come to you. Some of us need to listen to Jethro's advice. We need to stop trying to do it all and delegate what can be passed off.

Dear God, I am overwhelmed with everything that is on my plate. Give me wisdom as I seek to delegate some of these things. Amen.

Taught by God

"I will instruct you and teach you in the way you should go; I will counsel you with my eye upon you."
PSALM 32:8

In high school, my youth pastor was my mentor. He gave me opportunities to lead and teach the youth group. He would give me feedback on how I did and encouragement when I did particularly well. He would give me counsel when I was going through difficult things. In short, he kept his eye on me.

This is the promise that we have in Scripture; that God will keep His eye on us. He will teach us and lead us as we go through this life. If the task of leadership feels too heavy or burdensome, hold tightly to that promise.

Dear God, You are very gracious to keep Your eye on a sinner like me. Remind me of this, I pray. Amen.

Shepherd Leader

"With upright heart he shepherded them and guided them with his skillful hand."
PSALM 78:72

Shepherd leadership is the style of our God and the disposition of our Savior. It's what is prescribed for our church leaders to employ. Shepherd leadership is what we ought to aspire to in our various roles of leadership. So, what is shepherd leadership?

It's leadership with the rod and the staff. It's a mixture of guidance, protection, and correction. It's a leadership that understands where the green pastures are and how to get the sheep there. It's leadership with incredible patience and understanding that sheep can be stubborn and biting. This is the leadership we can only accomplish by the strength that God supplies.

Dear God, I want to be a shepherd leader. Give me the heart of a shepherd and the strength to lead in that way. Amen.

Keep Your Heart

*"Keep your heart with all vigilance,
for from it flow the springs of life."*
PROVERBS 4:23

Before we can lead anyone else, we must lead ourselves. If our hearts are tainted with sin, then we will lead others in that way. Where we struggle, we will fail to lead others towards success. So we must keep our hearts with all vigilance.

We cannot do this. We are so wracked with sin that we have no chance to be good enough to lead like we ought to lead. This is why we are perpetually dependent on the Gospel. Because Jesus is good enough and paid the penalty for our sin by His death on the cross, we can lead in His strength. Let's keep this perspective as we seek to grow in our leadership.

Dear God, I bring nothing to the table when it comes to being a capable leader. I am prone to selfishness. Help me. Amen.

Brainstorming

"Where there is no guidance, a people falls,
but in an abundance of counselors there is safety."
PROVERBS 11:14

Have you ever had the experience of thinking you have a great idea, and when you tell someone they think it's terrible? If you haven't, then either you're not sharing your ideas with enough people, or people aren't being honest with you! None of us have great ideas all the time. However, we often have decent ideas that can be turned into great ones through some counsel.

This is the wisdom of this proverb. Don't think through something in isolation. Surround yourself with trustworthy people that you can safely bounce ideas off of it. Your leadership and your life will be all the better for it.

Dear God, thank You for the faithful brothers and sisters You have put into my life. Lead me towards wisdom in my conversations with them. Amen.

Strive for Excellence

> *"Do you see a man skillful in his work? He will stand before kings; he will not stand before obscure men."*
> PROVERBS 22:29

Excellence is a worthy goal but a rotten idol. In whatever roles we find ourselves, we should strive for excellence. We should seek to do the very best that we can with God's help. To do anything less than that would be to strive to bring less glory to God for how He has used us.

However, the goal of excellence can become a wicked ruler. We must remember that the ultimate goal is the glory of God and the good of His people. While we are striving for excellence, that isn't the final goal. So when we do something that lacks excellence while striving for it, we aren't broken down or distraught. It's the striving the brings honor, not the final product.

Dear God, teach me to strive for excellence in all that I do. Let me do this for Your glory alone. Amen.

Lead with God

> *"fear not, for I am with you; be not dismayed, for I am your God; I will strengthen you, I will help you, I will uphold you with my righteous right hand."*
> ISAIAH 41:10

"I am with you." This is one of the promises that we see the most throughout the Bible. I think there is a great deal of purpose behind that. As believers, we are often going to feel isolated. We will struggle with doubts and feelings of weakness. We're going to find points of desperation where we will have no other option than to cry out to God.

God promises to be with us through all of this. And He repeats His promise to us over and over again because we are prone to forget it. I don't know the details of your life or what kind of struggle you may be going through. Take rest in the thought that God is walking with you and leading you through it.

Dear God, I feel alone and weak. Show me that You are with me through Your word and Your church. Amen.

Higher Ways

> *"For as the heavens are higher than the earth, so are my ways higher than your ways and my thoughts than your thoughts."*
> ISAIAH 55:9

What is the thing that you're the best at? Do you have an eye for photography? Are you the best shot at the range? Can you outwit anyone on trivia night? What is your greatest strength? Whatever it may be, we all know the reality that there is someone better. This is why world records are broken time and time again. While we may be the best for a season, we will never truly be the best.

This is not the case for our God. His ways are always higher than our ways, and His thoughts are always higher than our thoughts. If they weren't, then He would not be a very good God. Take a moment to praise Him today for truly being the best and being on your side as you walk through life.

Dear God, You alone are worthy of all praise and honor. I trust you with my life. Amen.

Called to Lead

> *"Before I formed you in the womb I knew you,*
> *and before you were born I consecrated you;*
> *I appointed you a prophet to the nations."*
> JEREMIAH 1:5

Consider this thought: before you were ever conceived, God knew you. He knew your life and how it would look. He knew the struggles you would face and how you would fail or overcome them. He knew your strengths and your weaknesses. And He called you anyways. He called you to lead your family, co-workers, and employees, knowing that you will do an imperfect job.

This is not a sign of God's trust in you. This is God letting you know that you can trust in Him. He knows you more intimately than anyone in your life. He wants to show you what it means to be a leader in your home, workplace, or local church. Get to know the God who knows you.

Dear God, You know me better than I know myself.
Reveal Yourself to me that I may know You better. Amen.

Found Working

> *"Blessed is that servant whom his master will find so doing when he comes."*
> MATTHEW 24:46

Speaking of His own return, Jesus uses the imagery of the relationship between a servant and his master. He brings to light the question of how the master will react to different servants. There will be a severe punishment to the servant who is found sleeping on the job or not doing his job at all. To the servant who is found doing worthy work, he will reward.

Let's strive to be found doing worthy work when our Master comes. Since we don't know when we cannot play the system or try to fool Him (as if we could). We have to be diligent, daily deciding that we will work as faithfully as we can that day.

Dear God, fortify my efforts and let me be found doing worthy work when Your Son returns. Amen.

Held Accountable

"Everyone to whom much was given, of him much will be required, and from him to whom they entrusted much, they will demand the more."
LUKE 12:48

This thought ought to strike a level of fear and humility into our hearts. We will be held accountable to an almighty God for our actions. He has called us to various roles and responsibilities in life. How we steward those responsibilities will be known by Him. Whether entrusted with a little or a lot, our Master is not one to be trifled with.

This should sober us on days when apathy or complacency begins to seem tempting. This should warn us when sin begins to grab hold of our hearts again. We will stand before the Judge of all creation and give an account for what we have done. Praise God that we will not stand alone but covered by the efforts of Jesus.

Dear God, sober me with this thought: that I will give an account to You for my actions and thoughts in this life. Amen.

The Goal of Leadership

"He must increase, but I must decrease."
JOHN 3:30

John the Baptist had a vast and growing ministry. People were coming from all over to hear him teach and to be baptized by Him. Jesus, Himself, was baptized by John the Baptist. After that moment, a shift began to take place. Fewer people were following John, and more people were following Jesus.

John's disciples came up to him and asked him what they should do about this issue. John's response was simple and profound, "He must increase, but I must decrease." This was the goal of John's leadership, to lead people to Jesus and not himself. Let that be our goal as well. However we're leading, let's lead others towards Jesus.

Dear God, Guide me in my leadership.
Allow me to lead others to Your Son. Amen.

⇒Day 259⇐

Pay Attention to Yourselves

> *"Pay careful attention to yourselves and to all the flock, in which the Holy Spirit has made you overseers, to care for the church of God, which he obtained with his own blood."*
> ACTS 20:28

This exhortation was originally given by Paul to the elders or pastors at a church he was working with. While not many of us are elders, we would all benefit from paying careful attention to ourselves. There are a few simple ways that we can do this.

The first is by reading God's word regularly. As it has been said, the Bible is the only book that reads you. Ask God to show you your sin and how to remove it. Secondly, pray. Pray that God would open your eyes to areas where you need to give attention and ask for strength to do so. Finally, find an accountability partner. Search for someone with who you can share your struggles and ask them to call you out lovingly in your sin.

Dear God, I cannot do this on my own. Help me to pay careful attention to my own life. Amen.

Lead with Zeal

"the one who leads, with zeal"
ROMANS 12:8

Zeal is a mixture of passion and vibrancy. When Paul instructs us to lead with zeal, he is after our heart motives and attitude. He wants us to lead in a way that shows we deeply care where we are going, and we are confident that we will get there.

So when it comes to leading your family financially, this means that you have a goal in mind and a plan to get there. It means that you're communicating these things lovingly to your wife or repentantly if your spending has been an issue in the past. Whatever area of your life you're needing to show more leadership, apply the zeal lens and see what direction that takes you.

Dear God, help me to be zealous in my leadership. Let me be zealous for biblical goals that glorify You. Amen.

Appointed by God

*"And he gave the apostles, the prophets,
the evangelists, the shepherds and teachers,"*
EPHESIANS 4:11

God has called us all to different tasks. Paul in 1 Corinthians uses the human body's illustration to describe how the church ought to function. Not all of us can be the eyes or the ears. We all have different functions that make up the full-body, of which Christ is the head. In that system, God has appointed some to fulfill different roles in church leadership.

Over the next few devotionals, let's think about what a church leader is to be doing and how we can support our church leaders in their efforts. Whether you aspire to be or have no desire to be, we are all involved with our church's leadership.

Dear God, You have gifted my church with wonderful leadership. Teach me how to support them in any way I can. Amen.

287

Equip the Saints

> *"to equip the saints for the work of ministry,"*
> EPHESIANS 4:12

The ministry of church leadership is to equip the saints. This is often confused in our church cultures. We can tend to think that the primary purpose of our leaders is to do ministry. While they are all called to minister, their primary ministry is equipping the church members to serve.

Let's let this truth change our outlook on our church leaders. Instead of asking why aren't they doing more, let's try asking what can we do to help? Thinking back to the body analogy, we need to be a part of the active body, not dying or unhelpful. There's no place for a hangnail Christian. Join in the work of ministry.

Dear God, I want to be a useful part of Your body. Send me on a mission at my local church to get involved and do the work of ministry. Amen.

Lead by God

> *"for building up the body of Christ,"*
> EPHESIANS 4:12

The goal of equipping the saints has a bigger goal in mind. It's for the sake of building up the body. We can think of it in terms of working out. If we never spend time going to the gym, running through the neighborhood, or walking downtown, then we can expect our bodies to get weaker and less healthy. If we commit to stretching our muscles and putting them to work, we can expect good results.

The same is true in church life. The leadership wants to equip the church members so that they will grow strong and healthy spiritually. Let's do our part in the body to pick up the slack that may encourage others to get involved.

Dear God, I want to be a part of a healthy body of believers working towards the same goals. Instill in me a passion for serving and building up the body. Amen.

Unified in the Gospel

> *"until we all attain to the unity of the faith"*
> EPHESIANS 4:13

When all of the members of the body of Christ are equipped, working together, and getting stronger, there is an undeniable unity that comes with it. The unity runs deep because it is centered around the faith that brought us together in the first place.

The work of the gospel is like a well. We go deeper and deeper into its depths, becoming closer and closer to those around us. The gospel is what saves us, brings us into the church, unifies us with our brothers and sisters, and sends us on a mission to bring others in. Our goal should be to venture further into this glorious truth.

Dear God, thank You for the deep unity that exists between the people at my local church. Let us rejoice in that this week. Amen.

Mature in Christ

> *"and of the knowledge of the Son of God, to mature*
> *manhood, to the measure of the stature of the*
> *"fullness of Christ,"*
> EPHESIANS 4:13

Maturity in Christ does not mean that we have it all figured out or that we're perfect. It means that we have a deep and continuing relationship with Christ to share with others in our lives. It means that we are ready to lead in some capacity, maybe even in the local church.

If you're not mature yet, ask yourself why? What is holding you back from taking steps forward? Where are your weaknesses, and how can you grow in those areas? Once you've determined some of those things, or if you need help doing so, build a relationship with someone who will pour into your life and help you grow.

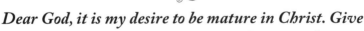

Dear God, it is my desire to be mature in Christ. Give me the grace necessary to grow in that way. Amen.

Content Leadership

> *"I know how to be brought low, and I know how to abound. In any and every circumstance, I have learned the secret of facing plenty and hunger, abundance and need."*
> PHILIPPIANS 4:12

Paul can truly write these words. As he pens them, he is sitting in a jail cell because of his unwavering commitment to preaching the gospel of Jesus Christ. Before his conversion, Paul was a successful Jewish leader who was on the fast track towards a valuable spot. He has felt the pride of success and the pain of struggle. He is well acquainted with both abundance and need.

Through all of the circumstances, Paul has remained content with his lot in life. Ultimately, he knows that these temporary things pale compared to the eternal weight of glory to come. This is his disposition as he leads the different churches he is involved with. We should strive to take up that disposition with God's help.

Dear God, teach me to be content with whatever my lot is in life. You're in control of it all. Amen.

Spine of Steel

*"for I did not shrink from declaring
to you the whole counsel of God."*
ACTS 20:27

There will be moments in our lives when we will need spines of steel to deliver hard truths to people who need to hear them. I'm thinking of moments when someone is caught in sin and wants to make various excuses to escape punishment. Perhaps you'll encounter a young woman wrestling with thoughts about abortion or an older man contemplating suicide. Whatever the situation is, we must not shrink back from declaring the word of God to them.

Two things I want to highlight about this thought: The first is that declaring God's word is done in love and gentleness. The second is that we are to respond with God's words and not our own. Our solutions will only cause more chaos for them. We must stick to wisely declaring God's word in any situation.

*Dear God, You have given us Your word to guide,
comfort, and confront us. Use it through me to do the
same for others. Amen.*

Imitate Their Faith

> *"Remember your leaders, those who spoke to you the word of God. Consider the outcome of their way of life, and imitate their faith."*
> HEBREWS 13:7

What does it mean to imitate the faith of your leaders? Faith isn't something you can see. It's not a physical action or process. It's something that resonates in our hearts. It's hard to even put words to it, let alone look at it to imitate it. What could the author of Hebrews mean?

Although we cannot see faith, we can see its effects on our lives. Like James said, "faith without works is dead." So when we look to our leaders, we ought to be able to see a life marked by faith. They trust God in difficult times, and they sing His praises in the good times. Their life is distinct from the world. Let's look for signs of faith and follow.

Dear God, You are the author and perfecter of our faith. Let me see that faith in the life of others. Amen.

Imitators of Me

"Be imitators of me, as I am of Christ."
1 CORINTHIANS 11:1

This is the essence of leadership and Christian discipleship. We are leading others as we are following Christ. We're not trying to make a name for ourselves or be seen as the greatest leader. We are trying to help others follow Christ as we follow Christ. It's as simple as that.

The question we need to wrestle with today is if we are worth imitating? Are we living a life that exemplifies what it means to follow Christ? If not, what are the areas that we need to grow in? Take a few moments today to ask yourself these questions and be ready to say to someone, "Be imitators of me, as I am of Christ."

Dear God, make me worthy of being followed.
Help me to walk more closely with Christ
as I seek to lead others. Amen.

The Reward of Leadership

> *"The one who conquers will have this heritage, and I will be his God and he will be my son."*
> REVELATION 21:7

What a beautiful reward or heritage we will have for our efforts here on earth. We will get God. Consider that! The infinite God of all nations desires to have a relationship with you. Not just any kind of relationship, but a Father-Son relationship. He wants to include you into His family. This is the great reward of leading others to follow Jesus. One day we get to be with Him.

But until that day, we have the precious gift of His Spirit indwelling us. We have a relationship with Him now that cannot be taken away. This should grow a longing for a better relationship, unaffected by sin because sin is no longer there. Ask God to give you a greater desire for that day.

Dear God, I want You. I want to be with You and live with You in perfect harmony. Thank You for Your Spirit. Amen.

Strong Men
Work

Work Heartily

> *"Whatever you do, work heartily,*
> *as for the Lord and not for men,"*
> COLOSSIANS 3:23

In this section of our study, we are going to take a long look at work. We will look at what it means to have a biblical work ethic and how that affects our lives. In Colossians 3, we have the best place to start as we begin this conversation.

With every verse we discuss, this will be the backdrop. All our work efforts are not ultimately for our boss, co-workers, families, or ourselves. We are ultimately working for the Lord. And if we keep that in mind, it'll greatly influence how we handle interactions with our boss, co-workers, and family. And so, let's strive to make this verse the theme of our work.

Dear God, I want to work heartily for You and for Your glory in all that I do. Give me that perspective today. Amen.

Inheritance from the Lord

> *"knowing that from the Lord you will receive the inheritance as your reward. You are serving the Lord Christ."*
> COLOSSIANS 3:24

Here we have another incredible promise to behold as we consider how we are to work in this world. Paul says that we will receive our inheritance from the Lord for our reward when we work heartily as unto him. If our reward is an inheritance from the Lord, then what exactly is that inheritance? The Bible teaches that when we believe, we are adopted into God's family. We are made sons or daughters. We share the privileges of being in the family with our Brother, Jesus. His inheritance is our inheritance.

There is a lot wrapped up in that statement, so I want you to take time to think through that. First, think about the incredible grace that goes into making us sons and daughters with those kinds of privileges. Second, consider what all Christ has been given by the Father and how we get to share in that.

Dear God, what a gift You have given us. Not only acceptance into Your family, but we are treated as sons and daughters. Amen.

Slothfulness

"Do not be slothful in zeal, be fervent in spirit, serve the Lord."
ROMANS 12:11

Slothfulness is an attitude that leads to inaction. You know someone is slothful based on how they act. The same is true for zeal. We know someone is zealous for something based on how they act. These two things are opposites. Paul exhorts us not to be slothful but zealous and fervent.

It's easy for us to slip into slothfulness. We are busy enough as it is. To add a level of spiritual discipline seems to make our day feel overloaded with responsibility. I want to challenge you to think differently about this. Christianity is not something you add to your day. It's a way in which you live your life. Instead of trying to add something to your schedule, allow the gospel to color your schedule.

Dear God. Help me to keep from slothfulness. Give me a passion and zeal for Your word. Amen.

Help the Weak

> *"In all things I have shown you that by working hard in this way we must help the weak and remember the words of the Lord Jesus, how he himself said, 'It is more blessed to give than to receive.'"*
> Acts 20:35

One of the specific jobs that we are given is to help the poor. We see God's heart throughout the Bible for those who are in physical need. We, too, need to adopt that mindset and foster that kind heart for those around us.

If you're thinking, "Where do I start?" I would begin by joining the work that someone else is doing. Don't feel like you have to make your own ministry and gather your own resources. Join in the work that God is already doing in different organizations. Go out and talk with different groups about how you can help and see if you align with theologically.

Dear God, You have called me to minister to the poor in some way, shape, or form. Show me the opportunities I should take. Amen.

Made for Good Works

> *"For we are his workmanship, created in Christ Jesus for good works, which God prepared beforehand, that we should walk in them."*
> EPHESIANS 2:10

We are the workmanship of Jesus. Like a carpenter making a chair, He has put us together for a specific use. What is our use? What is our purpose? This verse teaches us that we were made for good works. We were made to honor God by doing the good works that bring Him glory.

There are a lot of things that fall under that category. From a concerned phone call to wisely calling the shots, we are to be about good works. Use this thought as a filter for what you spend your time doing. If we're created for good works, then what are we wasting our time doing?

Dear God, reveal to me what things in my life are not good works. What can I shed doing so that I may do what I'm meant to do? Amen.

Do Not Grow Weary

"And let us not grow weary of doing good, for in due season we will reap, if we do not give up."
GALATIANS 6:9

Doing worthy work is weary work. It takes effort to think through our lives and fine-tune our schedules for the glory of God. It takes giving up getting to do some of the things that we would enjoy serving someone else. It may take giving up some alone time to be in the presence of someone who is hurting. Being godly takes work.

Don't grow weary, brother. There is a harvest coming. One day we will reap the benefits of all of the hard work. One day that friend who needs salvation will understand the gospel like never before. One day that ensnaring sin will release its grip on you. Until then, work hard and do not grow weary.

Dear God, I am weary of this work. Strengthen me and uphold me today. Amen.

Abounding in the Work of the Lord

> *"Therefore, my beloved brothers, be steadfast, immovable, always abounding in the work of the Lord, knowing that in the Lord your labor is not in vain."*
>
> 1 CORINTHIANS 15:58

Can you confidently say that you are abounding in the work of the Lord? It's hard to quantify what that means, and I won't try to do that here. But a life abounding in the work of the Lord has intentionality to it. It has a great deal of selflessness baked in. It is a life that is confirming situations into ones that will do someone spiritual good.

Let's start pressing ourselves in that direction. Let's seek to live a life described as abounding in the work of the Lord and not merely abounding in work. Be busy doing what is worth doing for the glory of God.

Dear God, I confess that my life is not abounding in Your work. Guide me towards this abundance. Amen.

Devoted to Good Works

> *"The saying is trustworthy, and I want you to insist on these things, so that those who have believed in God may be careful to devote themselves to good works. These things are excellent and profitable for people."*
> TITUS 3:8

We are to be devoted to good works. That begs the question, "What are good works?" The nomenclature can be a little misleading. Good works are not anything that is deemed good by society. Some negative actions, like punching someone, can be good if done in defense of another.

Here are two things that make an action good. First is if that action has been deemed good by the Father. Examples of this would be bearing one another's burdens or showing humility and kindness. Secondly would be the intent behind your actions. If your motivation to act is out of a love for God and His people, then it is likely that you'll be doing good works.

Dear God, help me to be someone who is devoted to good works. Let me know your word and have pure intentions. Amen.

⇒Day 279⇐

Weak Hands

> *"But you, take courage! Do not let your hands be weak,
> for your work shall be rewarded."*
> 2 CHRONICLES 15:7

Asa, faced with the daunting task of bringing about spiritual reform to the nation of Israel, was understandably feeling weak and unable to do the work. The prophet Azariah spoke the words above to encourage Asa to continue on in work.

We, too, will have days where our hands are weak, and our hearts are tired. Let's hear the words of Azariah afresh today. The work we are doing is difficult, yes. But it is work worth doing and work that will be rewarded in the end. Take courage, brother.

Dear God, I am feeling overwhelmed and too weak to carry on. Strengthen my hands to continue in the work You've called me to. Amen.

Average Joe

"and because he was of the same trade he stayed with them and worked, for they were tentmakers by trade."
ACTS 18:3

Maybe you're reading these devotionals and thinking, it's easy for these men to say to be devoted to good works. That's all they do! They are pastors and missionaries. They are kings of God's people. They don't have average jobs and live a typical lifestyle. Let me encourage you with the life of the great pastor, missionary, and apostle Paul.

Paul was a tentmaker by trade. Yes, his life was extraordinary in many different ways. But Paul knew what it meant to be your average Joe, just living life. He knew how to be that average Joe used for God's glory each and every day. Join in with all the tentmakers and average Joe's who are working hard for God.

Dear God, there's not much special about me, but there are innumerable things special about You. Help me to highlight those things today. Amen.

Gospel Saturated

> *"Let the thief no longer steal, but rather let him labor,*
> *doing honest work with his own hands, so that he may*
> *have something to share with anyone in need."*
> EPHESIANS 4:28

In Ephesians 4, Paul talks about the radical change of heart and behavior that happens for the one who has placed their faith in Jesus. This change is typified by the concept that we don't only do good for us, we do good for others. It displays an abundance of grace and care for those around us.

In this example, Paul says that the sinner saved by grace not only gives up thievery and begins honest work, but he works to give to others. This is the full effect of the gospel in our lives. Our honest work is not just for our families or us. It is for the benefit of those around us so that they might believe in the gospel, too.

Dear God, radically change my heart and my actions so that I can be witness to the goodness of Your gospel. Amen.

Eternal Work

> *"Do not work for the food that perishes, but for the food that endures to eternal life, which the Son of Man will give to you. For on him God the Father has set his seal."*
> JOHN 6:27

Working for today is important. We have to be fed, clothed, and sheltered to survive in this world. Many of us have families to support or parents to care for. Working for temporal things is not wrong in and of itself. However, when we become fixated on the temporal, idols begin to form.

This is why we're encouraged to keep our minds on the eternal things that come from Jesus. There are souls and eternities on the line every day that we go to work. We should let that govern how we work and how we conduct ourselves while on the job.

Dear God, forgive me for where I have allowed the temporal to overshadow the eternal. Adjust my priorities. Amen.

Establish Our Work

> *"Let the favor of the Lord our God be upon us,*
> *and establish the work of our hands upon us;*
> *yes, establish the work of our hands!"*
> PSALM 90:17

I want to challenge you to pray this prayer regularly. We should pray that the Lord would establish the work of our hands. This means that as we work, the Lord works in and through us. This kind of prayer will keep us thinking of the work that we are doing.

When we pray for the Lord to establish our work, we ask that He guide what we do. We are praying that He would empower us to do the work well. We are seeking for Him to confirm and use the work that we are doing for His glory. This is no light prayer that we find in Psalm 90. Pray it wholeheartedly today.

Dear God, I pray that You would establish the work of my hands and make it fruitful for Your glory. Amen.

Worthless Pursuits

> *"Whoever works his land will have plenty of bread,*
> *but he who follows worthless pursuits lacks sense."*
> PROVERBS 12:11

I love to play games on my phone. Recently, I have been reliving childhood memories by playing old games that I used to play on a handheld device before the smartphone revolution. I have spent hours finishing quests and saving princesses. There are times in my day where these pursuits have interfered with my job productivity and even my ability to focus on my family.

When those moments come, what was for my relaxation and entertainment has morphed into a worthless pursuit. Be wary of worthless pursuits in your life. There is value in having hobbies or avenues of stress relief, but we cannot let those things overshadow our worthy goals: love our God, family, and neighbors.

Dear God, thank You for the gifts of entertainment.
Help me not to pursue them as I do You. Amen.

Unsatisfied Sluggard

> *"The soul of the sluggard craves and gets nothing,*
> *while the soul of the diligent is richly supplied."*
> PROVERBS 13:4

The mental picture that is painted for us in this proverb is shocking. The soul of the sluggard is like a starving and weak animal begging for just a bite. The soul of the diligent is like a mighty lion, full of strength and vigor. The irony here is that the sluggard is physically saving his energy while spiritually wasting away.

Be cautious when dealing with the temptation of slothfulness. It promises a coming vigor and vitality that it cannot produce. Even on difficult days, trust the working hard without overworking is God's design for us and our souls.

───⁂───

Dear God, I admit that I am tempted to become like a sluggard. Remind me of the importance of hard work for my soul's sake. Amen.

───⁂───

Ruler or Ruled

> *"The hand of the diligent will rule,*
> *while the slothful will be put to forced labor."*
> PROVERBS 12:24

The goal of Solomon in this proverb is not to distinguish between leaders and followers. Everyone has a God-given natural tendency towards one or the other. The point here is to show the effects of diligence. Those who are diligent will have control over their lives. Those who are lazy will have their lives controlled by them.

We are all under the sovereign reign of our God, but He has ordered our lives in such a way that we are responsible for managing it. Like Adam in the Garden of Eden, we are given a lot to steward. So, how are you stewarding what God has given you? Who are you allowing to steward those things in your place?

Dear God, You have entrusted me with various things in my life. Grow me into a diligent manager of those things. Amen.

⇒ Day 287 ⇐
Mere Talk

> *"In all toil there is profit, but mere talk tends only to poverty."*
> PROVERBS 14:23

Don't just talk about it, be about it. That's a phrase that one of my good friends used to say all the time. For him, it wasn't enough to say, "Let's get lunch sometime," or, "I'll do better next time." He pushed that lunch would happen or that there would be action steps to be better next time.

This is the thought behind this proverb. Mere talk does not profit us. We cannot be men that just talk about what we would like to do. It's time for us to do it. Stop talking about how you want to read your Bible more. Read. Quit going on about how you wish you had a more vibrant prayer life. Pray. Don't just talk about it, be about it.

Dear God, do not let my words be mere talk. Give action to my words and strength with every step. Amen.

Provide for Your Household

> *"But if anyone does not provide for his relatives, and especially for members of his household, he has denied the faith and is worse than an unbeliever."*
>
> 1 Timothy 5:8

Paul holds nothing back when speaking about those who choose not to provide for their household or relatives. Paul is not talking about those in circumstances that make them unable to provide. He is calling out those who are living a selfish lifestyle that leaves behind those closest to them. He says that these are the actions of those who do not know Jesus.

You see, Jesus gave everything for His household. He gave His life so that we could be adopted as His brothers and be brought into His family. If this is the way of our Lord, it should be the way of our lives. Providing for our family is essential to our jobs and a reflection of the gospel.

Dear God, lead me away from my selfishness. Let me see the selfless Christ and behold His kindness. Amen.

First Share

> *"It is the hard-working farmer who ought to have the first share of the crops."*
> 2 TIMOTHY 2:6

My favorite part of cooking is that I get to eat as I go. I get to sample the individual ingredients and taste the dish as it's developed. This means that I am inevitably the first to taste the final product of all the hard work. Paul suggests that this simply makes sense. The person who puts in the work ought to be the person who first reaps its benefits.

This should press us in two ways. The first is more obvious. We should strive to put in the work because there is a natural reward for doing so. The second is that we only get the first share. This implies that there are other shares that we have worked for and others get to benefit from. Let's let this shape how we view the goal of our hard work.

Dear God, You have given me a job that serves me and those around me. Use this for your glory and our good. Amen.

Origin of Work

> *"The Lord God took the man and put him in the garden of Eden to work it and keep it."*
> GENESIS 2:15

Work is a good thing. It is a part of the perfect design of God. Before Adam and Eve ever sinned, they were given a job: tend to the garden. This means that work is not a part of the curse that came when humanity sinned in the beginning.

Perhaps for you, this is a difficult concept to wrap your mind around. Maybe you find no joy or fulfillment in the work you do. The work you do may be mind-numbing or painful. In the next session, we will discuss why that is. For now, ask God to give you a holy appreciation for work.

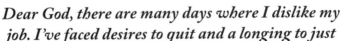

Dear God, there are many days where I dislike my job. I've faced desires to quit and a longing to just stay home. Help me to appreciate the perfect plan that You have for me. Amen.

By Sweat

> *"By the sweat of your face you shall eat bread,"*
> GENESIS 3:19

If work was a part of the original design of God, then why is it so difficult? Why does it seem so unfair at times where some barely work and get all the profits? What is so perfect about work? The issue is not with work but with the effects of sin.

Part of the curse that God placed on humanity due to their disobedience was that we would eat "by the sweat of our face." Elsewhere it says that our gardens (or workplaces) would be full of thistles and thorns. The difficulty of work should grow in us a longing for Jesus to return and make all things right again.

Dear God, work is hard. It's hard because of the sins that I have committed. It's hard because this world is sinful. Come quickly, Lord Jesus. Amen.

Day 292

Lottery Lifestyle

> *"Wealth gained hastily will dwindle, but whoever gathers little by little will increase it."*
> **PROVERBS 13:11**

There are a few ways to gain wealth hastily. The only commendable one in the Bible is through hard work and God's blessing, you see a great increase in profitability or given a generous gift. Neither of these things is what Solomon is writing about here.

The quick reward he is speaking of is wealth that is gained dishonestly or without any work. This could be done by stealing some sort of putting all your funds into a lottery or betting system. Neither of those things is the desire of God. The natural consequence of funds gained in this way is that they will not last.

Dear God, winning it big in the lottery or stealing a little off of the top would be an easier way to get ahead. Show me the fallacy of that temptation. Amen.

Enjoy Your Work

> *"also that everyone should eat and drink and take pleasure in all his toil—this is God's gift to man."*
> ECCLESIASTES 3:13

Some of us have the blessing of being able to enjoy the work that we do. If you've been able to find a job in a field that you're passionate about, do not take that blessing for granted. Not everyone can say the same for themselves.

For others who are doing a job that we didn't grow up hoping we would become, what are we to do? How can we find enjoyment in it? Make efforts to enjoy knowing that you're a part of something bigger than yourself. You're providing either another job for someone or a product for another by you doing your job. No matter what role you play, your work is necessary for the whole production to take place. Look for moments like this to find some joy.

Dear God, I confess that I have asked what the point of it all is. I feel frustrated at work and not joyful. Remind me of how You're using my work to provide for others. Amen.

Watch Yourselves

"Watch yourselves, so that you may not lose what we have worked for, but may win a full reward."
2 JOHN 1:8

You have probably heard the story of the turtle and the hare. They enter a race against each other. The hare speeds off at the beginning, earning a sizable lead. He then takes time to eat a snack and take a nap, comfortably ahead of the turtle. During his snoozing, the turtle continues to plod along, ultimately winning the race.

One of the issues with the hare was that he became complacent before the race was over. We must watch ourselves. The race is not over. There is still work to be done for the kingdom of God. Let's continue to race on until we cross the finish line.

Dear God, I want to run my race well. Give me strength and endurance to keep going strong. Amen.

Better Together

> *"Two are better than one, because they*
> *have a good reward for their toil."*
> ECCLESIASTES 4:9

This is a simple truth: two are better than one. Two people working together towards the same goal means that they reach that goal faster than either one could on their own. This means that it would be wise for us to seek out our number two. Who can we link arms with to accomplish our goals?

This truth will play out differently for various areas of your life. At work, you need someone with the same work philosophy. In marriage, you need a partner who is going in the same direction you are. At church, you need to link arms with brothers that believe in the same God you do. Two are better than one.

Dear God, in the Trinity, I see this beautiful truth played out. As the Father, Son, and Holy Spirit, You are working amongst Yourself to bring about my good and Your glory. Amen.

Eye-Service

*"not by the way of eye-service, as people-pleasers,
but as bondservants of Christ, doing the
will of God from the heart,"*
GALATIANS 6:6

There ought to be a distinction between the way followers of Jesus work and how the average person in the world works. The distinction lies in the sincerity of the actions. The world would have us offer a way of working that is just eye-service or people-pleasing. They would suggest that working only when the boss is looking is acceptable.

Whether the boss is in view or not, our God is watching how we work. This is because we are ultimately working for Him. Let's serve as bondservants of Christ. From sincerity of heart, we ought to work in a manner that is worthy of our efforts.

*Dear God, I am tempted to be a people-pleaser
more than I am a God, please. Set my heart
on the right path. Amen.*

Master Kindness

> *"Masters, do the same to them, and stop your threatening, knowing that he who is both their Master and yours is in heaven and that there is no partiality with him."*
> GALATIANS 6:9

The simplest way to ensure a servant does what you want is to threaten them with punishment or death. Fear will drive them to work. But this is not a healthy relationship or one that honors God. This is now how God chooses to relate to us. Instead of inflicting us with paralyzing fear, He approaches us with grace. He desires that we serve Him out of our love for Him, not our fear.

If you're in a position of power, don't use fear to drive your workforce. Rather, inspire your people to love and trust you. Not only will you get better and longer effort from your people, but you'll also be mirroring a God that they desperately need a relationship with.

Dear God, You have given me this position of authority. Teach me to wield it in kindness, not with fear. Amen.

Strong Men

Honor

Honored by God

> "*Therefore the Lord, the God of Israel, declares:
> 'I promised that your house and the house of your father
> should go in and out before me forever,' but now the Lord
> declares: 'Far be it from me, for those who honor me I will
> honor, and those who despise me shall be lightly esteemed.'*"
> 1 SAMUEL 2:30

If you're like me, you felt a little uncomfortable reading those words, that we would be honored by God. Who are we to deserve any honor from a holy and righteous God? He has graciously saved us from our sin and poured the wrath due to us on His Son. What honor could there be for us?

The honor spoken of here is honoring the covenant promise that God made the Israelite people. God is saying to His people, yet again, I will keep my promise to you. He says that to us today, too. If you are in Christ, you are a part of the people of God and receive the benefits of those promises.

*Dear God, what an amazing thought that You
would make such a promise to me, a sinner!
I will rejoice in You today. Amen.*

Honoring God

> *"To the King of the ages, immortal, invisible, the only God, be honor and glory forever and ever. Amen."*
> 1 TIMOTHY 1:17

In this short exaltation, we are given four reasons to honor our God. The first is that He is the king of the ages. This is saying that He has been and will continue to be the King of kings. No other king can say that their rule extends from age to age. Secondly, He is immortal, meaning that He cannot die. Thirdly, He is invisible. No creature can make that claim. Finally, he is the only God.

While many may try to claim His name or portray His power, there is only one God. This God alone deserves all honor and glory forever and ever! His name is Jesus, and He is our savior!

Dear God, You are worthy of all honor, glory, and praise. To You alone do I give my life. Amen.

327

Honorable Marriage

"Let marriage be held in honor among all, and let the marriage bed be undefiled, for God will judge the sexually immoral and adulterous."
HEBREWS 13:4

I f you're single, there is a way you can honor your wife, even before you meet her. That's by honoring your future marriage by keeping your marriage bed undefiled. What that means is that you will save yourself physically for your wife to be. Anything in the realm of sexually immoral or adulterous would dishonor your wife before and during your marriage.

The reality is that many of us have fallen short in this area and have failed to honor our wives as we should. There is grace for you, brother. Repent of those sins and believe in Jesus' name for forgiveness. Work through the messiness of what that sin may have caused and trust in your God.

Dear God, I want to honor my wife before and during my marriage to her. Lead me on a path of sexual purity. Amen.

Honor Your Father and Mother

> *"Honor your father and your mother, as the Lord your God commanded you, that your days may be long, and that it may go well with you in the land that the Lord your God is giving you."*
> DEUTERONOMY 5:16

For some of us, this is a difficult command to follow. Maybe that's because your parents were absent during your childhood. Perhaps your parents were present but abusive or neglecting. Maybe it was never a dangerous situation, but you and your parents simply don't see eye to eye on many things. How do we keep God's word in these scenarios?

The answers will vary on how to go about it, but let me give you these things to think through. You can honor your parents by not obeying them when they ask you to do what is sinful. You can honor your parents by seeking to forgive them for the hurt they have caused you. You can honor your parents by being a testimony of the greater Father we have in our God.

Dear God, show me how to honor my father and mother. I thank You that You are the perfect heavenly Father. Amen.

329

Honor Authority

> *"Let every person be subject to the governing authorities. For there is no authority except from God, and those that exist have been instituted by God."*
> ROMANS 13:1

The basis for our allegiance to the different authorities in our lives is not in their goodness. We can all attest to some form of authority that is corrupt or at least has corrupt individuals in it, giving it a bad name. And yet, the command is for us to put ourselves into subjection before them. Why?

God has full and final authority. Nothing will be done here on earth that isn't ultimately a part of God's sovereign plan for our lives. Also, God has instituted those in authority. He is the one who ultimately puts those men or women in their place. This does not mean that God approves of their actions, but we must remember that He is sovereign over all things. Therefore, as far as it doesn't contradict the will of God, we must submit to our authorities.

Dear God, You are the highest and best authority there is. Help me to trust in Your sovereignty as I submit to the authorities in my life. Amen.

Honor Pastors

> *"Let the elders who rule well be considered worthy of double honor, especially those who labor in preaching and teaching."*
> 1 TIMOTHY 5:17

The term "elder" in the New Testament is used synonymously with "pastor" or "bishop." When Paul tells Timothy to consider the elders worthy of double honor, he is speaking about pastors. He presses the point and says that those who labor in preaching and teaching are especially worthy of that honor.

Paul suggests that we honor our pastors by financially supporting them, especially those who regularly teach the congregation. But the honor of our pastors should not be limited to finance. We should honor them by respecting their authority and encouraging them regularly. They pour so much effort and love into us. The least we can do to honor them is to love them and their families in return.

Dear God, thank You for the spiritual leaders that You have put in my life. Use me to encourage and honor them this week. Amen.

Honorable in All Things

> *"Pray for us, for we are sure that we have a clear conscience, desiring to act honorably in all things."*
> HEBREWS 13:18

It is not always easy to act honorably. We will be faced with challenging circumstances that will strain our faith and tempt us towards poor behavior. We may be tempted to lash out in anger or withdraw in fear. Neither of those actions is honorable.

This is why the author of Hebrews asks for prayer. As he faces challenging situations in his life, he knows that he will need the strength that only God can provide to act honorably in all things. Brothers, let's pray for one another. Let's lift each other up in prayer to the only God who can supply that kind of strength.

Dear God, I pray for all of my brothers and sisters in Christ who are going through difficult times. Strengthen them so that they can act honorably for Your sake. Amen.

Honorable Wealth

*"Honor the Lord with your wealth and
with the firstfruits of all your produce;"*
PROVERBS 3:9

Whether we have plenty or little, we are called to honor the Lord with our wealth. What are some guidelines for how we can honor the Lord with our wealth? Solomon gives us one of those answers in this proverb. We can honor him with the firstfruits of what we have.

This means that we cannot give God the leftovers in our lives. We intentionally set aside our assets for His use on the fiscal period's front end instead of the end. And this isn't limited to money. Some of us are wealthy with time or gifts. We ought to set those aside for God's use as well.

*Dear God, I want to honor You with what You have
blessed me with. I commit to setting it aside for
Your use and Your glory. Amen.*

Cleansed of Dishonor

> *"Therefore, if anyone cleanses himself from what is dishonorable, he will be a vessel for honorable use, set apart as holy, useful to the master of the house, ready for every good work."*
> 2 TIMOTHY 2:21

At the time that I am writing this, it has been raining for days on end. Finally, there was a break in the clouds, and my son could go outside to play for a few hours. When he came inside, he was filthy. Where there is an abundance of rain, you'll find an abundance of mud. He decided to bring most of that mud inside with him. He needed to be cleansed.

This is all how we come before God. We are filthy with sin in desperate need of cleaning. To the glory of His great name, He is gracious and merciful to cleanse us by the sacrifice of His Son, Jesus. Take time to rejoice in this truth today. We have been perfectly cleansed by our sinless Savior.

Dear God, although I did not deserve it, You have cleansed me from the inside out. Help me to live like I've been cleansed. Amen.

Dust Yourself Off

> *"So flee youthful passions and pursue righteousness, faith, love, and peace, along with those who call on the Lord from a pure heart."*
> 2 TIMOTHY 2:22

Although we have been cleansed by the Son and are positionally right before the Father, we still deal with the grime of sin in our lives. That's why we are told, even now, to flee from our youthful passions. Not only to flee from sin but to run towards what is clean and holy.

This is a beautiful exchange that we get to make as believers. We get to trade the filth of sin for the beauty of faith, love, and peace. We can do this from a pure heart by His grace. We are bound to get dirty from time to time, but we no longer have to stay in our filth. Dust yourself off and pursue righteousness.

Dear God, don't give up on me. Continue to clean me off and use me for Your purposes. I want to pursue what is good. Amen.

Full Honor

> *"Honor everyone. Love the brotherhood.*
> *Fear God. Honor the emperor."*
> 1 PETER 2:17

Peter leaves no room for excuses. He begins by saying that we should honor everyone. There are no loopholes in that statement. Everyone means everyone, from those that we love to those that we are tempted to hate. Honor everyone.

But then he gives two specific groups. Honor your brothers and sisters in Christ by loving them and honor those in political authority. Why pinpoint those groups among everyone that we are to honor? These people play a special role in the advancement of the gospel. We need our spiritual family to link arms with. And we need to honor our governments in such a way that allows us to freely spread the gospel.

Dear God, teach me what it means to honor everyone.
I confess that there are people in my life that
I struggle to honor. Amen.

Given Honor

> *"And no one takes this honor for himself, but only when called by God, just as Aaron was."*
> HEBREWS 5:4

Honor is not something that can be taken. It must be given. This means that we hold great power. We can bless someone so greatly by giving them that they cannot get in any other way. We cannot buy honor or steal it from another.

So, ponder this question today. Who have you given the honor to recently? Who is in your path that you can bless by honoring this week? We have such a great ability to give our brothers and sisters grace by honoring them in different ways. Let's strive to do that this week.

Dear God, it is such a privilege to be able to honor others. Put honorable people in my path and show me how to give honor. Amen.

Finding Honor

> *"Whoever pursues righteousness and kindness will find life, righteousness, and honor."*
> PROVERBS 21:21

In the last session, we talked about the great privilege of giving honor. This time, let's take time to think about how to be given the honor. What kind of person is given honor? This proverb makes it really clear. Whoever pursues righteousness and kindness.

Righteousness is whatever is good and right. Kindness is doing whatever is good and right and a loving and gentle way. Those who deserve honor are those who have been fully transformed by the gospel, both in their actions and their approach. May God make us honorable men.

―――――⸎―――――

Dear God, I want to be an honorable man. Lead me on a path of righteousness and kindness. Amen.

―――――⸎―――――

Honor with a Promise

> *"Honor your father and mother" (this is the first commandment with a promise),*
> EPHESIANS 6:2

In the Ten Commandments, there is one that comes with a promise. The command that tells us to honor our father and mother is connected with the promise of a long life. While giving honor is a great gift to the honored, there is a reward for the giver.

This is how God has designed His Law. It is the design of the way that life works the best. Don't forget the promises that are attached to the difficult commands. God has His ways and His purposes in mind for everything in our lives, especially His commands for us.

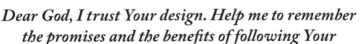

Dear God, I trust Your design. Help me to remember the promises and the benefits of following Your commands. Amen.

Day 312

Blood Bought Honor

> *"for you were bought with a price.*
> *So glorify God in your body."*
> 1 CORINTHIANS 6:20

Brother, never let this fact escape you. You were bought with a price. Specifically, the price was the death of the Son of God. He shed blood in your place. His perfect life accounted for your record. His suffering that you deserved. You were bought at such a high and costly price.

If this is true, what else can we do that glorify God in our bodies? How else could we spend our lives than to honor Him with every moment that we can? We have this incredible opportunity to use our days repaying Him for His inexhaustible kindness.

Dear God, I cannot thank You enough for the price You paid for me. I want to use my life to show You how appreciative I am of that. Amen.

Honor Elders

> *"You shall stand up before the gray head and honor the face of an old man, and you shall fear your God: I am the Lord."*
> LEVITICUS 19:32

God calls us to honor the elderly. It can be easy to overlook the elderly or even dismiss their thoughts and their opinions. If you're younger, you can view their opinions as outdated or lacking understanding of today's world. I want to urge you to honor the elderly.

See them for the wisdom that they offer. See them as the brothers and sisters that they are. See them as mentors for you in the faith. Elderly saints are an incredible gift to the church. Let's seek to honor them and learn from them lessons that we cannot learn any other way.

Dear God, there are many elderly people that You have placed in my life. I want to give them the honor that is due them. Amen.

⇒ Day 314 ⇐

Honor to Whom It's Owed

> *"Pay to all what is owed to them: taxes to whom taxes are owed, revenue to whom revenue is owed, respect to whom respect is owed, honor to whom honor is owed."*
> ROMANS 13:7

Our God is one of justice. He operates in such a way that He will always do what is right and just. He will give to whoever what they are owed, and He will demand what He is owed. This character found in our God is seen in how He teaches us to live our lives.

We are to give to others what they are owed. Whether it is payment, taxes, income, respect, or honor, if they have earned it, we are to give it. This is right. This is just. We should strive to live a life that is a right reflection of the character of our God.

Dear God, You are righteous and just. I praise You that this is always true of You. Teach me to reflect on that in my life. Amen.

Humility Comes Before Honor

> *"The fear of the Lord is instruction in wisdom, and humility comes before honor."*
> PROVERBS 15:33

It will be impossible for us to honor someone if we are not humble. Humility allows us to open our eyes and see the truth about ourselves and other people. It allows us to notice how sinful and flawed we really are. In other words, we can then see how unhonorable we truly are.

Once we have taken our focus off of ourselves, we will appreciate other people all the more. We will see areas where others are stronger than us. That won't drive us to jealousy, but to the right honoring of how God has made and grown them. Let's seek God's help in becoming humble.

Dear God, I am prideful and have a hard time thinking of others before myself. Graciously and gently humble me. Amen.

Honor your Wife

> *"Likewise, husbands, live with your wives in an understanding way, showing honor to the woman as the weaker vessel, since they are heirs with you of the grace of life, so that your prayers may not be hindered."*
> 1 PETER 3:7

Whether or not we honor our wives affects our relationship with them and our relationship with God. Notice the final section of this verse. Honoring our wives keeps our prayers from being hindered. Why is that? Because dishonoring our wives is dishonoring our sister in Christ. It's an offense against a family member and ultimately an offense against the Father.

So how can we honor our wives? We can seek to understand them. Truly knowing someone, their shortcomings, and their successes is one of the greatest ways to honor someone. It takes time, effort, and humility to dive into someone's life and not look away at the ugly parts.

Dear God, you have seen and known me and have not looked away. Help me to honor my wife in this way. Amen.

Endless Honor

"And I heard every creature in heaven and on earth and under the earth and in the sea, and all that is in them, saying, "To him who sits on the throne and to the Lamb be blessing and honor and glory and might forever and ever!"
REVELATION 5:13

What a beautiful picture of God's people that we get a glimpse of in the book of Revelation. John is imprisoned on the isle of Patmos when the Holy Spirit gives him a vision of the end. There he sees multitudes of God's people singing His praises.

More specifically, he sees a lamb that looks as if it has been slain being called worthy to open the scroll. This is a picture of our Lord, who was sacrificed for us. All honor or all of eternity is directed towards Him. He alone is worthy of that kind of eternal praise.

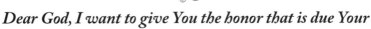

Dear God, I want to give You the honor that is due Your name for all of my days, either here or in Heaven. Amen.

False Honor

> *"And the Lord said: "Because this people draw near with their mouth and honor me with their lips, while their hearts are far from me, and their fear of me is a commandment taught by men,"*
> ISAIAH 29:13

In this verse, the Lord brings a judgment against Israel. He says that they honor Him with their lips, but their hearts are far from Him. In other words, they say all the right things and even do all the right things, but their heart motivation is off.

It's not enough to just say and do what is honoring to our God. He knows us intimately. He can peer into our souls and see the very core of who we are. He knows when we're just trying to put on a show. Take off the mask and genuinely offer honor to our God.

Dear God, I have tried to deceive You. Foolishly, I have thought words or actions in and of themselves are what you desire. Amen.

Honor Your Boss

"Let all who are under a yoke as bondservants regard their own masters as worthy of all honor so that the name of God and the teaching may not be reviled."
I TIMOTHY 6:1

Have you ever had a difficult boss? I've had my fair share of bosses who didn't appreciate the work done for them or didn't delegate responsibilities properly. Some of you had bosses who treated you poorly or fired employees without just cause. When we are under the "yoke" of our employer, we are told to honor them.

Why? What good does it do to honor our bosses when they are undeserving? Paul says it is "so that the name of God and the teaching may not be reviled." Here is the reality. Your employer ought to know that you're a Christian. How you react to them will be a witness to your God and what your Bible teaches. Bear that in mind.

Dear God, I want to be a good witness to you in difficult situations. Help me to honor my boss even if they are not worthy of it. Amen.

⇒ Day 320 ⇐

Honor Christ

> *"but in your hearts honor Christ the Lord as holy, always being prepared to make a defense to anyone who asks you for a reason for the hope that is in you; yet do it with gentleness and respect,"*
> 1 PETER 3:15

The Bible has been clear that we are to honor Jesus Christ as our Lord. And we have many ways of doing that. Peter here gives us an example. He says that we can honor Christ as Lord by always being prepared to share our testimony.

This means that we need to have thought through how we should explain our testimony to someone. This also means that we have to be looking for opportunities to share what God has done in our lives with other people. Take time to think if you're ready for those things? Are you able to share your testimony? Are you looking for those opportunities?

Dear God, You have called me to be ready to share my testimony when the opportunity presents itself. Prepare me. Amen.

Honor the Trinity

"that all may honor the Son, just as they honor the Father. Whoever does not honor the Son does not honor the Father who sent him."
JOHN 5:23

In this passage of Scripture, we get a vital piece of information about Jesus. We are taught that we are to honor Him in the same way that we honor the Father. This is pointing us to the truth that Jesus is God as the Father is God. He is worthy of the eternal honor that the Father is due. Although they are different persons, they are the same God.

The Trinity is a complex idea that we cannot fully comprehend. However, we must take in its implications. We have one God who exists in three persons, the Father, the Son, and the Holy Spirit. This God is worthy of all the praise and honor we can muster. Where there are questions about the Trinity, supplement them with praise for His holiness.

Dear God, I do not understand all of who You are. Help me to appreciate that more than I question it. Amen.

Despise His Name

> *"A son honors his father, and a servant his master. If then I am a father, where is my honor? And if I am a master, where is my fear? says the Lord of hosts to you, O priests, who despise my name. But you say, 'How have we despised your name?'"*
> MALACHI 1:6

We have another example of what dishonor looks like. Previously, it was that their words were right, but their hearts were off. Now, God is bringing this indictment. They have despised His name. Let that sink in for a moment. The people of God that have been miraculously saved and graciously led to a Promised Land have despised the name of their God.

We've been there too. We've been mad at our God for circumstances in life. We have doubted His goodness or maybe even His existence. We have not represented His name well in our actions with our co-workers. We have in many senses despised His name. Where there should be shame on us, we have been covered by His grace and mercy.

Dear God, forgive me for despising Your name. Thank you for the never-ending grace and mercy that You show to me. Amen.

Honor Your Word

> *"Let what you say be simply 'Yes' or 'No';*
> *anything more than this comes from evil."*
> MATTHEW 5:37

If you say you're going to do something, then do it. That's the simple message of this verse. We cannot spend time adding qualifiers or "what if's" to every commitment in life. Let your "yes" be "yes" and your "no" be "no." If we spend our time providing loopholes for ourselves, we will never be trustworthy.

If we're never trustworthy, then we cannot make disciples. We cannot lead someone to follow Jesus if they are unsure if they can trust what we say. There is great damage to be caused by someone who is always backing out of commitments. Sometimes, this is unavoidable. But generally speaking, if you say you're going to do something, make every effort to do it.

Dear God, help me to honor the commitments that I make. I want to be known as someone who is trustworthy. Amen.

Strong Men

Rest

God Rested

> *"So God blessed the seventh day and made it holy,*
> *because on it God rested from all his work*
> *that he had done in creation."*
> GENESIS 2:3

We have discussed a lot in this book together. We have seen countless ways that we need to be strong in the Lord and in the strength of His might. We have been given various commands to follow and attitudes to hold. We have been challenged to grow in every way.

For our final major section, let's take some time to appreciate what it means to rest. We get this concept primarily from how God rested on the seventh day of creation. After He had finished what He was doing, He rested. This is significant because He doesn't need rest as we do. And yet, He made it a point in Scripture to say that the regular flow of His work included a measure of rest.

Dear God, Help me as I study these next few days to understand what biblical rest looks like. Ultimately, teach me to rest in You. Amen.

Jesus Rested

> *"After making purification for sins, he sat down at the right hand of the Majesty on high"*
> HEBREWS 1:3

Once again, we see this example, but I want us to look at it in a different light. Like the Father, Jesus did not need to rest. He is God. However, He still chooses to sit down as if to say the work is done. Jesus did say this before His death. He cried out from the cross that it is finished.

Here we find the essence of our rest as Christians. We are to rest in the finished work of Christ. What He has done to make purification for our sins puts us in a position to spiritually rest. We can stop trying to be good enough or holy enough. The work has been done. Rest in Christ today, brother.

Dear God, what a simple and profound truth!
I can rest in the finished work of my savior.
Help me to savor that today. Amen.

Jesus Gives Rest

> *"Come to me, all who labor and are heavy laden,*
> *and I will give you rest."*
> MATTHEW 11:28

Over the next few sessions, we're going to take a look at the type of rest that can be found in Jesus. First, let's notice who the rest is offered to. All who will come and all who are heavy laden. Without a doubt, we are all those who labor. We all go through difficult times and challenging circumstances. We are weighed down by stress, anxiety, and social pressures.

But it is only those who come to Jesus who will find rest. We must reach a point in our lives where we give up carrying the load by ourselves, and we turn to Him for help. The great thing about our Lord is that for all those who will come, He gives rest.

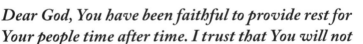

Dear God, You have been faithful to provide rest for Your people time after time. I trust that You will not turn me away. Amen.

Take My Yoke

> *"Take my yoke upon you, and learn from me,*
> *for I am gentle and lowly in heart,*
> *and you will find rest for your souls."*
> MATTHEW 11:29

A yoke is a piece of wood that is designed to be carried on your shoulders. It can be used to carry buckets of heavy material, allowing the load to be placed on your back and not your arms. A yoke is given to a servant by his master.

Jesus is not offering just His yoke, but His lordship. When we come to Him to find rest, He offers us His yoke in a paradoxical way. The lordship of our Saviour is characterized by His nature. He calls himself gentle and lowly in heart. He is a kind of good master. His yoke is not one to be feared.

Dear God, I accept Your lordship, and I take Your yoke for myself. Use me however You see fit. Amen.

My Yoke Is Easy

> *"For my yoke is easy, and my burden is light."*
> MATTHEW 11:30

The burdens of this world are too much to bear. We have all kinds of people to please. Our families have expectations. Our jobs have requirements. We have personal goals that we cannot even seem to reach. This world has no rest to offer us. It is a terrible master.

Jesus' lordship offers an easy yoke and a light burden. How is this possible? He has done the work for us. Our performance no longer rides on our shoulders but on His. As we go through this life in faith, we are resting and working out of the work that He has accomplished.

Dear God, Your yoke is easy, and Your burden is light. Allow me to experience that new life in Christ. Amen.

The Lord Is My Shepherd

"The Lord is my shepherd; I shall not want."
PSALM 23:1

Psalm 23 is one of the most well-known and loved psalms in Scripture for a very good reason. It helps us put into words the struggles of this life and the incredible comfort and peace we have while knowing God. It is simply a beautiful psalm. Let's take time to fully appreciate it over the next few devotions.

It begins by setting the stage for the whole psalm. It paints the picture of God as our shepherd who faithfully provides for His sheep. In this imagery, God is portrayed as the provider and protector of His people who are ultimately helpless without Him. It is because of His love for His sheep that He continues on in His work.

Dear God, You are a good shepherd who loves me. Because of who You are, I can confidently say that I shall now want. Amen.

Led to Rest

> *"He makes me lie down in green pastures.*
> *He leads me beside still waters."*
> **PSALM 23:2**

The first action mentioned about our shepherds is that he leads us towards rest. Notice the locations. He leads us towards green pastures. This is where there is plenty of good food to eat. It is so rich and full that we can lay down and enjoy it.

He also leads us to still waters. This word picture puts a peaceful scene in our minds and shows yet another provision: water. When our Shepherd is near, we have nothing to fear and nothing to want. We're fully taken care of under the loving and watchful eye of our good God.

Dear God, the way You lead me towards rest is incredible. Help me to experience that today. Amen.

He Restores My Soul

> *"He restores my soul. He leads me in paths of*
> *righteousness for his name's sake."*
> PSALM 23:3

If you were unsure of the shepherd's ability to care for you, this verse would put those worries to rest. Here is the promise: He restores your soul. What more could we ask for? Not only has He said He would provide for our wants and lead us towards peace. But He will restore our very souls.

This action sets us on the path of righteousness. Because of His restorative work in our hearts, we can live rightly for Him and for His name's sake. He does all of this so that we will go on and write our own psalms that tell of His goodness and sing of His mercy. Take time today to tell His goodness to someone or journal a poem that reflects His kindness to you.

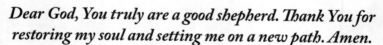

Dear God, You truly are a good shepherd. Thank You for restoring my soul and setting me on a new path. Amen.

I Will Fear No Evil

> *"Even though I walk through the valley of the shadow of death, I will fear no evil, for you are with me; your rod and your staff, they comfort me."*
> PSALM 23:4

There are three things that the psalmist finds comfort in the valley of the shadow of death. First is the presence of his shepherd. This makes sense because even if we don't know the way, our shepherd always does.

However, the next two things are a little strange. He says that the rod and the staff of the shepherd comfort him. Here's why. The rod and staff are representative of protection and correction. The staff would help guide the sheep along while the rod was used to ward off wolves. In and of themselves, the rod and staff are of no comfort at all. But in the hands of a good shepherd, there is little more comforting than them.

Dear God, Your rod and Your staff comfort me still today. In Your word, You provide direction and protection. Amen.

My Cup Overflows

> *"You prepare a table before me in the presence of my enemies; you anoint my head with oil; my cup overflows."*
> PSALM 23:5

King David, the one writing this psalm, was well acquainted with enemies. Many times in his life, someone attempted to kill him, even his own son. He literally shared a table with his enemies at times.

Even so, note what David says. He says that God anoints his head with oil, and his cup overflows. These are both signs of blessing from God. Even during trials, God blesses David and sets him apart in front of his enemies. This is not because David is special or deserving. Remember, David is but a sheep in this analogy. This is because God, his shepherd, has set His love on him.

Dear God, You have set Your love on me and have blessed me in more ways than I realized. Thank You. Amen.

⇒≫Day 334≪⇐

I Will Dwell

> *"Surely goodness and mercy shall follow me all the days of my life, and I shall dwell in the house of the Lord forever."*
> Psalm 23:6

In light of all that he has meditated on, David comes to this conclusion of hope. He says he will surely be followed by goodness and mercy and that he will dwell with God forever. One theologian has said that it was like goodness and mercy were nipping at his heels, following wherever he would go.

Brother, this is our great hope too. We have this future to look forward to. We have eternity in the presence of our Savior King on the horizon. As we walk towards that glorious end, we will be trailed by His goodness and mercy all the days of our lives. What better way to rest in God's provision for us than to consider the means and the end of our salvation.

Dear God, I am amazed at the kindness You have chosen to show to me. I am a sheep, desperately in need of You. Amen.

⇒ Day 335 ⇐

Rest a While

> *"And he said to them, "Come away by yourselves to a desolate place and rest a while." For many were coming and going, and they had no leisure even to eat."*
> MARK 6:31

Jesus regularly took time to get away to a peaceful place to rest and pray. He would invite His disciples to do this as well. They were so busy that they barely had time to eat, the Bible says. That's not good for them or for their ministry. Seeing their need for rest and escape, Jesus offered it to them.

We need to be aware of our need for rest and escape. It can be hard to remember that the world will go on without us for a few hours or even a few days. We need to make an intentional effort to get away for some rest from time to time. Do not let work, even good work, consume your life, leaving you dry or depleted for your family.

Dear God, You offer me daily spiritual rest. Help me to seek out physical rest as often as I need it. Amen.

God Gives Sleep

> *"It is in vain that you rise up early and go late to rest, eating the bread of anxious toil; for he gives to his beloved sleep."*
>
> PSALM 127:2

The psalmist brings a hard word for anyone who struggles with being a workaholic. He says that it is vain to get up early and go to bed late to eat the bread of anxiety. Surely, he is not referring to those who have to live this way. If that's the only way you can make ends meet for your family, then work hard and provide. But for those who choose this lifestyle because we are chasing money or power, he says we are chasing a pointless goal.

He takes it a step further than to deny yourself sleep for money to deny yourself a gift from God. He is the one who gives His people sleep. He gives His people physical and spiritual rest as often as they need it. He will not leave us to waste away. Take that gift gladly.

Dear God, I trust You with my family and my finances. Give me to rest tonight. Amen.

God's Presence

> *"And he said, "My presence will go with you, and I will give you rest.""*
> EXODUS 33:14

Moses had a daunting task before him. He had already led God's people out of bondage to Egypt and towards the Promised Land. He had journeyed with them through the wilderness and faced non-stop grumbling and complaining. Now he was nearing the Promised Land and the transition of power to go to Joshua.

Moses was leading an immature and rebellious people on an impossible journey. He had much to be anxious about. However, God promises him rest with His presence. God was going to travel with them by pillar of cloud and fire. He was going to meet with Him in the tent of meeting as they went. Moses had nothing to be anxious about because his God was going before Him. We have the same promise given to us today.

Dear God, thank You for Your presence in my life. Allow me to experience that presence anew today. Amen.

Dwell in Safety

> *"In peace I will both lie down and sleep;*
> *for you alone, O Lord, make me dwell in safety."*
> PSALM 4:8

Where does your rest come from? In what do you find security and peace of mind? Maybe it's in your financial standing. Perhaps you're well equipped to defend your home in the case of an intrusion. Whatever it is, does that thing surpass your confidence in God?

Financial security and home defense plans are good things to have. They are gifts from God. But we must remember just that. They are from God. It is God who ultimately gives us security. The psalmist here says that God makes him dwell in safety. God puts him in that position to be able to lie down and sleep. Trust God today. He will keep you safe in the best way.

Dear God, You are my shield and my security. All of my peace and comfort ultimately come from You. Amen.

Be Still

> *"Be still before the Lord and wait patiently for him; fret not yourself over the one who prospers in his way, over the man who carries out evil devices!"*
>
> PSALM 37:7

How hard is it for you to be still? I am someone who likes to get things done. I do not like to wait for something to come to me. I want to go out and get it. So, when the Bible talks about being still and waiting patiently for God, I have a hard time obeying those directives.

Being still allows us to do a few things. It gives us a moment to stop and think about how God has been faithful thus far in our lives. It gives us a chance to look around and see how God is working in the lives of those around us. And it gives us time to look ahead in the promises that God has made to us. Take time to be still today.

Dear God, I confess that it is not easy for me to be still. Slow me down and show me the goodness of being still. Amen.

Pray About Everything

> *"do not be anxious about anything, but in everything by prayer and supplication with thanksgiving let your requests be made known to God."*
> PHILIPPIANS 4:6

Do not be anxious about things. Sure, Paul. Whatever you say! This seems like an impossible command to keep. There are countless things in our lives to be anxious over. How could anyone keep from being anxious about anything?

First, let's acknowledge that anxiety and concern are different. Concern means you're thinking about someone or something, but you're trusting God to handle it. Anxiety means you're no longer trusting God. So how can we remind ourselves to trust Him when times are stressful? Pray, thank God, and let Him know what's on your mind. He will take care of the rest.

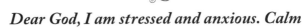

Dear God, I am stressed and anxious. Calm my fears and help me to trust You fully. Amen.

Peace of God

> *"And the peace of God, which surpasses all understanding, will guard your hearts and your minds in Christ Jesus."*
> PHILIPPIANS 4:7

If we deny our anxieties and pray to God in trusting obedience, He gives us a promise. The promise is a peace that passes understanding. Maybe you've had the pleasure of experiencing that peace. It truly is hard to communicate because we cannot fully understand it.

Paul goes on to say that this peace will guard our hearts and minds. Once we have given our anxieties over to Him, we can find rest in this peace because this peace protects us. It keeps us at peace when we are in the midst of it.

Dear God, I cannot fully understand it, but I am so thankful for Your peace. Keep me in perfect peace. Amen.

⇒Day 342⇐

Remember the Sabbath

> *"Remember the Sabbath day, to keep it holy."*
> EXODUS 20:8

When God led His people out of Egypt by His servant Moses, He gave them the Law. This law is essentially summarized by the Ten Commandments. The Fourth Commandment is our verse for today. God commanded His people to rest weekly. For the Israelites, this was to take place on Saturday. They were not to do any work on that day; they just rest and worship God.

For many Christians today and for centuries beforehand, Sunday is their day of rest and worship. Whether your schedule affords a Sunday or a Thursday, be sure to set aside a day of rest and worship for you and your family.

Dear God, You have commanded that Your people take time to rest. You know how desperately I need it and how easily I will neglect it. Amen.

Saved in Rest

> *"For thus said the Lord God, the Holy One of Israel, "In returning and rest you shall be saved; in quietness and in trust shall be your strength." But you were unwilling,"*
> ISAIAH 30:15

God's people are being called to repentance in the book of Isaiah. They have given their love to idols that they have made and have angered their God. God, being full of mercy and grace, offers a chance for repentance. He says that in returning to Him and resting in Him, they will be saved.

This salvation for them was both from a physical threat in their enemies and a spiritual threat in His wrath. While we may not have enemies to worry about, we will still find salvation from God in God. If we will repent and trust in Him for our soul's rest, we will be saved. Will you be unwilling?

Dear God, I am willing and ready to trust You. Lead me in repentance and towards rest. Amen.

The Better Sabbath

> *"So then, there remains a Sabbath rest for the people of God."*
> HEBREWS 4:9

While the Fourth Command was given to the Israelites, all of the commands of God have been fulfilled in Christ. This begs the question, how should a Christian live? Are we still under the law? Specifically, are we still to keep the Sabbath command.

The answer is, "Yes." There still remains a Sabbath rest for the people of God. However, our Sabbath rest is found ultimately in Jesus. It is not in keeping the Law or being good enough for God. Jesus has done those things for us. We can rest in His perfection.

Dear God, You sent Your Son to give us a Sabbath rest that is greater than before. Show me that rest. Amen.

Find Rest

> "Thus says the Lord: "Stand by the roads, and look, and ask for the ancient paths, where the good way is; and walk in it, and find rest for your souls. But they said, 'We will not walk in it."
> JEREMIAH 6:16

Where will we find our rest? What path can we take to get there? There is not a new path to be forged or a new method to be tried. We walk in a good way. A way that is an ancient path. For centuries, generations after generations, faithful Christians have gone before us. They have left countless examples for us to follow and learn from.

My encouragement for you today is to pick up an old book. Read the biography of men like William Carey, Charles Spurgeon, Martin Luther, or Saint Augustine. There is so much that we can glean from the great writings and lives of these men. Do not neglect the ancient path. It is a good way.

Dear God, thank You for the examples that You have given in these faithful men of old. Teach me from their lives. Amen.

Rest is Sweet

"If you lie down, you will not be afraid;
when you lie down, your sleep will be sweet."
PROVERBS 3:24

Rest is sweet. It is soothing to the soul. It can be so sweet that you'll exhale a sigh of relief as you lie down. Rest is all the more sweet when you can lay your head on the pillow at night without any fear.

As God's people, this is our reality. We have a sovereign King who reigns over all creation. There is nothing that escapes His sight and nothing that is outside of His control. We are the only people that can claim such a fearless rest. Take a moment tonight as you lay your head down to sleep to thank God for this sweet slumber.

Dear God, I have nothing to fear, for You are my God.
Let me experience the sweetness of rest tonight. Amen.

Sabbath for Man

> *"And he said to them, "The Sabbath was made for man,*
> *not man for the Sabbath."*
> MARK 2:27

In the utter depravity of our hearts, we can turn the great gift of rest into a draining task. This is what the Pharisees did. They questioned Jesus' actions on the Sabbath day. He would heal men and feed His disciples on the Sabbath. You see, the Pharisees were so concerned with keeping the Law that they added their own laws as safeguards. This left them working so hard and missing the point of the Sabbath day.

Jesus reminds them and us that the Sabbath is for us. It is a gift from God. Do not spend all your energy stressing about keeping the Sabbath day. Yes, do it. But do not let it be a taskmaster over you. It is there to give you rest, not to put you to work.

Dear God, help me to enjoy the Sabbath. It was given to me as a gift, not a burden. Amen.

Jesus Gives Us Peace

> *"Peace I leave with you; my peace I give to you.*
> *Not as the world gives do I give to you. Let not your*
> *hearts be troubled, neither let them be afraid."*
> JOHN 14:27

Could there be a sweeter peace than what Jesus has? Being God Himself, He has never caved to fear or spent a sleepless night worrying over what tomorrow will bring. He lives in perfect peace with God, others, and Himself. This is a peace that truly passes our understanding.

This is also the peace that He promises to give to us: His peace. He says that there is nothing in the world that can compare to the peace that He offers. No amount of money, power, or respect can bring the calm of Christ to us. Ask for Jesus to give you that peace that makes all matters fade into the background.

Dear God, I need Your peace. I have tried to drown out my troubles with many things. Only You can bring true peace. Amen.

For God Alone

> *"For God alone my soul waits in silence;*
> *from him comes my salvation."*
> PSALM 62:1

I think it is interesting that the psalmist says that his soul waits in silence. We read through the psalms and see that their writers are anything but silent. We read passages of Scripture that encourage us to make our request known to God and to cast all our cares on Him. Where is this silent soul that he is speaking of?

I think the silent soul comes after all you can say has been said. You've cast your cares. You've made your requests known, and now all there is to do is wait. Silently. Patiently. Wait. This is not something a restless soul can do. But ours can be at rest, knowing that it is God alone who can offer us the salvation we seek.

Dear God, silently I wait for You. Amen.

He Does Not Grow Weary

> *"Have you not known? Have you not heard?*
> *The Lord is the everlasting God, the Creator of the ends*
> *of the earth. He does not faint or grow weary;*
> *his understanding is unsearchable."*
> ISAIAH 40:28

The Lord is an everlasting God. This means that there was no beginning, and there will be no end to our God. He will not run out of steam, and His battery will not need to be recharged. Or, as the prophet Isaiah says it, "He does not faint or grow weary."

We can rest in our God because He is an infinite source of energy. There is no amount of stress that we can cast on Him that will tire Him out. He is abundantly able to handle all of the problems in our lives and then some. Rejoice in this everlasting God today!

Dear God, You are from everlasting to everlasting.
There is no end to what You can do for me.
Give me rest in that. Amen.

He Gives Power

> *"He gives power to the faint, and to him who has no might he increases strength."*
> ISAIAH 40:29

Taking His promise of rest to His people a step further, He will give power to those who are faithful. As we are physically, emotionally, mentally, and spiritually exhausted, we can choose to rest in our God. But not only can we trust to receive rest, but renewal as well.

Are you seeking your renewal in the Father? Or are you searching after mind-numbing television or pain-numbing medicine? Be careful of these good things that God has given us. They are no replacement for Him and His renewal. Notice your choices today when you need a pick-me-up. Where do you run?

Dear God, I want to run to You for my strength throughout the day and my renewal at night. Amen.

We Will Grow Weary

> *"Even youths shall faint and be weary,*
> *and young men shall fall exhausted;"*
> ISAIAH 40:30

We are not unstoppable. We will grow faint. Even at the prime of your life, there was a breaking point for you. Whether you were an incredible athlete or had unmatched mental stamina, eventually, you grew tired. This is human nature.

This is a design of God in our lives. It is a constant reminder to us of our desperate need of Him. We will always be dependent on Him. This is so we will remember to worship Him and give Him the glory due to His name. Our frailty, as frustrating as it can sometimes be, is for our good and His glory.

Dear God, I am tired, and I thank You for it.
You use it to remind me of You. Amen.

⇛Day 353⇚

Renewed Strength

> *"but they who wait for the Lord shall renew their strength; they shall mount up with wings like eagles; they shall run and not be weary; they shall walk and not faint."*
> ISAIAH 40:31

This promise of renewed strength is given to those who wait for the Lord. Our tendency is to take matters into our own hands or to leave matters altogether. We either fight for what we want, or we take flight. We embrace, or we escape. What the Bible calls us to do is wait. Wait for the Lord.

This isn't a passive waiting where we do nothing. And there is no waiting that requires us to get up and go. This is awaiting that is actively trusting that whatever God has planned is the best thing. This is awaiting that is preparing for the next step. Like the Israelites sleeping in their sandals before the Exodus, we should be ready to go.

Dear God, I am not good at waiting. Help me to trust and prepare as I wait for the next thing You have for me. Amen.

He Cares for You

> *"casting all your anxieties on him,*
> *because he cares for you."*
> 1 PETER 5:7

This verse contains a truly astounding truth. It's not so much that we can cast all our cares on Him. We can cast our cares on a lot of people. Maybe you've had someone randomly break down on you and lay out all of their issues before you. The issue when that happens is we don't truly care about that person or their problems. We may feel bad for a moment, but we don't deeply care.

This cannot be said about our God. When we cast our cares on Him, we can trust that He is not just nodding along, waiting for the conversation to be over. No. He cares for you. Truly and deeply, He has an honest love and compassion for you. So share. Share your sorrows and your worries. Cast all your anxieties on Him, because He cares for you.

Dear God, I cannot express to You how much it means to me that You care. Thank You for being so gracious. Amen.

A Handful of Quiet

"Better is a handful of quietness than two hands full of toil and a striving after wind."
ECCLESIASTES 4:6

Ecclesiastes is a book that Solomon wrote to determine the meaning of life. He explored all that life had to offer and contrasted it with his relationship with God. He came to many profound conclusions, one of them being balance. Life needs to have balance.

This is true even when it comes to work and rest. On the one hand, we can hold our work and responsibilities. On the other hand, we must hold onto our rest. Otherwise, we will end up with empty hands that are striving after wind. Finding and keeping that balance can be a difficult thing to do. Ask someone to hold you accountable and examine your life with you to figure this out.

Dear God, You hold all things in the right balance. Help me to examine my life and to do the same. Amen.

Return to Rest

"Return, O my soul, to your rest; for the
Lord has dealt bountifully with you."
PSALM 116:7

If this verse does not bring a smile to your face, you have clearly not taken it in. The Lord has dealt bountifully with you. He has given you more than you have asked for; more provision, more grace, more mercy. Our God, whose resources will never run dry, has chosen to set His love on us and deal bountifully with us.

So, when our souls feel stirred and troubled. When they want to rise from their rest, call them back. Preach the gospel to yourself and remind your soul of their reason to rest. It is not in your abilities or in the perfect world around you. Our souls find rest in an inexhaustible God.

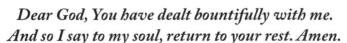

Dear God, You have dealt bountifully with me.
And so I say to my soul, return to your rest. Amen.

The Lord Sustained Me

> *"I lay down and slept; I woke again, for the Lord sustained me."*
> PSALM 3:5

Here in this verse, we get another picture of our utter dependence on God. While we sleep, the Lord sustains us. Think about it. While you're sleeping, you're not making yourself breathe. You're not keeping yourself out of danger. You're not doing anything that makes you stay alive voluntarily. The Lord is sustaining you.

So whether you're away and going or you're in a deep sleep, you're fully dependent on the Lord. He is the one who gives us rest, and He is the one who wakes us from our slumber every morning. We owe literally everything to our God.

Dear God, You sustain me in ways that I have yet to discover. Your kindness is unsearchable. Amen.

Satisfy the Weary

> *"For I will satisfy the weary soul, and every languishing soul I will replenish.""*
> JEREMIAH 31:25

A good diagnostic question to ask yourself or a friend is, "How's your soul?" Not, "How are you doing?" It is easy to dodge that question with a simple, "I'm good." Half of the time, we do not even consider our response when asked that question.

Let's ask a question that will cause ourselves and our friends to think. How is your soul? Is it happy, resting, and trusting in God? Is it lost, unsure of where to go? Is it weary from a difficult day, week, or life? However your soul is, our unchanging God makes this promise to you. He will satisfy your soul and replenish it.

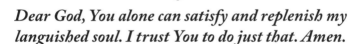

Dear God, You alone can satisfy and replenish my languished soul. I trust You to do just that. Amen.

Strive to Rest

> *"Let us therefore strive to enter that rest, so that no one may fall by the same sort of disobedience."*
> HEBREWS 4:11

It is almost an oxymoron how the author of Hebrews words this verse. Strive to enter that rest. How can you strive for rest? Is not striving the opposite of resting? Let's remember that resting in God is not us doing nothing. It's us putting in the work of trusting. It's us placing our anxieties and temptations aside, knowing that God has everything under control.

Putting in that trust takes striving. It takes active steps on our part to make it happen. There is no passivity for the Christian. Take a step today. Spend some time in prayer confessing your inability to trust. Share this struggle with a trusted friend. Read God's word that constantly points us towards trust in Him.

Dear God, I am striving to enter the rest You have for me. Carry me along as I go towards this goal. Amen.

Strong Men

in the Lord

In Christ

> *"Therefore, if anyone is in Christ, he is a new creation.*
> *The old has passed away; behold, the new has come."*
> 2 CORINTHIANS 5:17

For our final few devotionals together, I want to remind us of the big picture here. What it means to be strong in the Lord and in the strength of His might. A common phrase repeatedly found in the New Testament is "in Christ" or "in Him." This is a descriptor of who we are. We are in Him. This is where we find our strength, our new identity in Christ. Let's finish by looking at some of the "in Christ's" we find in scripture.

The first is that we are a new creation in Christ. What a glorious truth. We are not the sin-strangled men we were before. We are new people with a new directive. We have been made new and given new strength.

Dear God, by Your grace, You have made me a new creation. Give me the strength that comes with that gift. Amen.

In His Death

> *"We were buried therefore with him by baptism
> into death, in order that, just as Christ was raised
> from the dead by the glory of the Father,
> we too might walk in newness of life."*
> ROMANS 6:4

To be in Christ means that we share in everything that He is. When Christ died, we died with Him. While His death was physical, we died to our sin. When we place our faith in Him, we reap the benefits of His death, so it is just as if we died. It is as if we paid that penalty for our sins.

A picture of this death that we share is in the act of baptism. If you are a Christian and have never been baptized, I want to strongly encourage you to pursue that. Talk to your pastor and ask about the steps you need to take to do so. It would be in obedience to Christ and in the representation of your unity in His death.

Dear God, I am so thankful for the death of Your Son. It accomplished so much for me and set me free to live. Amen.

In His Resurrection

> *"For if we have been united with him in a death like his, we shall certainly be united with him in a resurrection like his."*
> ROMANS 6:5

As we know and trust, Christ's life did not end in death. He was raised from the dead by the mighty hand of our God. So if we share in His death, we also share in His resurrection. We have a new life that He was given. We are no longer under the penalty of death, nor do we have to wallow in it. We have been given a new, resurrected life.

One day we will experience this resurrection in a fuller way. If we die before Jesus comes back, the Bible teaches that we will be physically resurrected from the dead in likeness with Jesus. We will be given a new, glorified body like our Savior. And we will live with Him for all of eternity.

Dear God, I long for that day of resurrection. Until it comes, help me to fully appreciate the resurrected heart You have already given me. Amen.

In His Kingdom

> *"But our citizenship is in heaven, and from it,*
> *we await a Savior, the Lord Jesus Christ,"*
> PHILIPPIANS 3:20

In Christ, we are given new citizenship. We are no longer primarily citizens of whatever country we reside in. We have been grafted into a new kingdom. We are under a new ruler. He is King Jesus and His dominion in a heavenly one. We are invited to be citizens of that kingdom.

Until He returns or He calls us home, we live in-between state. We are not fully getting the privileges of His kingdom, nor are we allowed to neglect it. It is like we are ambassadors on a mission from His kingdom as we walk in our physical nation now.

Dear God, living in the in-between is difficult some days. I long to go home to Your kingdom. Amen.

He Strengthens Me

> *"I can do all things through him who strengthens me."*
> PHILIPPIANS 4:13

After studying what it means to be strong in the Lord, I hope to feel this verse's full weight. This is not a catchy slogan for a Christian sports team. This is not just a cool phrase to have printed on an athletic shirt. This is the gospel applied to the Christian life.

Because Jesus lived a perfect life, died a sacrificial death, and was raised victoriously from it, I can do all things. Because the all-powerful God emptied Himself and became a man to suffer in my place, I can do all things. Because it is an infinite God on whom I rely for all my strength, I can do all things. Brother, rejoice. Again I say, "Rejoice!"

Dear God, what a privilege it is to know and be known by You! Give me strength, I pray. Amen.

In His Victory

> *"But thanks be to God, who in Christ always leads us in triumphal procession, and through us spreads the fragrance of the knowledge of him everywhere."*
> 2 CORINTHIANS 2:14

In Christ, we are given victory. As if on parade with him walking through the town square, we enjoy the benefits of His victory for us and over us. He has not allowed sin and death to reign any longer. He has taken His rightful seat on the throne and has been crowned the ruler of all. As Paul says elsewhere in his letter to the Corinthians, "O death, where is your sting? O, death, where is your victory?" Jesus has won the battle for your heart. All that is left to do is for us to acknowledge Him as our Lord and follow Him with our lives. Have you done this? Have you entrusted your life in the hands of our Victor? If not, I urge you, after all, we have understood in our study together, trust Jesus. He is the only rightful king.

Dear God, You have won the victory! Today, I walk in boldness and confidence because of what Your Son has accomplished for me. Amen.

BLESS YOU

Made in the USA
Columbia, SC
03 May 2024